Scriptural Marriage

Scriptural Marriage

A brief study of 1 Corinthians 7

Thomas Pierre Verduyn

iUniverse LLC
New York   Bloomington

SCRIPTURAL MARRIAGE
A BRIEF STUDY OF 1 CORINTHIANS 7

iUniverse books may be ordered through booksellers or by contacting:

iUniverse LLC
1663 Liberty Drive
Bloomington, IN 47403
www.iuniverse.com
1-800-Authors (1-800-288-4677)

ISBN: 978-1-4401-7525-1 (sc)
ISBN: 978-1-4401-7526-8 (e)

Printed in the United States of America.

iUniverse rev. date: 05/05/2014

Preface to the Reader

The purpose of this little book is to examine "Scriptural marriage." The intent is to look plainly at what the Bible teaches about marriage, answering ordinary questions like: Who should marry? When can they marry? How should one find a spouse? Is divorce allowed? When is remarriage acceptable? And so forth.

The Lord Jesus spoke to his disciples, saying, "You are the salt of the earth." (Mt 5:13). Is it possible, at least to some degree, that the governments of the Western world are struggling to redefine marriage because the Christian church, having lost its own understanding of Scriptural marriage, has thereby lost its salty savour? I pose this question because of a firm belief that a sober study of the Bible forces us unquestionably to answer in the affirmative.

What does the Bible teach about marriage? The plan of this book is to answer this question by a somewhat thorough examination of the seventh chapter of the apostle Paul's first letter to the church in Corinth. Besides the fact that this chapter provides a wealth of information about marriage, it has also proved to be a source of much confusion and a refuge for many false doctrines about marriage. So it will be useful to study this chapter.

I hope that the reader will not discredit this book, though he discover that my own life is not in order in regard to marriage. Indeed, from early youth I had been taught and had accepted many of the errors that are exposed in the following pages. It is not surprising, therefore, that my own struggle in understanding Scriptural marriage has been intense. I offer this book to the Christian community not because my life is in order, nor because I have any new or keen insights into marriage, but because God has declared things to us in the Bible and these things need to be boldly affirmed. It is my hope and earnest prayer that this book many be used of God so that many are spared from the errors I and others have fallen into.

Part of the difficulty in studying what the Bible teaches about marriage is that our cultural view of marriage is so different from Scriptural practices that it becomes a challenge to understand what Scripture means. In my case, the gloss over my eyes began to fade as I studied the history of the Jews, and of the Christian church. I now realize that the way that churches in North America view marriage is a recent phenomenon, at the most 350 years old. Is the new better? Was the old rejected on scriptural grounds? What is the source of the revolution? What does the Bible really teach?

The conclusions I was forced to make by what I found in the Scriptures, and in the history of the church, are startling. Indeed, when I even begin to share my findings, people almost universally call me *extreme*. Nevertheless, since a return to Biblical marriage is so fundamentally required in the church, I offer this book to the reader, encouraging you to read and study, and to compare all things with the Scriptures. And I urge you to be open to what God's holy Word really says about marriage.

It is hoped that the reader will not immediately cast off the book when something contrary to his understanding is encountered. Rather, the reader is encouraged to give careful attention to the Scriptures, and to prayerfully ponder what you read here. It is strongly recommended that the book be read at least in its entirety before passing judgment on it. I have earnestly prayed and sought to present only the truth as it is found in the Scriptures. And I think that warrants the attention of every believer.

The reader will soon discover that I have chosen to use the King James Version (KJV) in quoting the Bible. The fact that this translation has remained so popular for the past 400 years, and that it has done so in spite of major changes in the English language, in spite of many competing translations in the early 1600's, and in spite of multiple new translations since, is clear evidence that the KJV was an excellent translation. I do not deny that recent and general changes in the English language have rendered the KJV awkward and confusing to the average reader. Nor do I deny that many of the now archaic forms found in the KJV have the possibility of misleading the reader. Nevertheless, to avoid the appearance of novelty by means of new and fresh translations of old and familiar Scripture, I have chosen to adhere to the KJV.

There is enough apparent novelty in the content of this book, that I deemed it dangerous to simultaneously stray from the time-honoured KJV. Yet, the reader will notice that reference is repeatedly made to the Greek text to clarify the true meaning of the Scriptures. My sympathies, then, to those that are unfamiliar with the KJV. And I encourage such to make whatever extra efforts might be required to understand the Bible texts here quoted.

Thomas Verduyn, March 2009
Carman, Manitoba

Table of Contents

CHAPTER 1

Singles and Newlyweds

What does the Scripture teach about marriage? I invite the reader to consider this important question by turning to the seventh chapter of the apostle Paul's first letter to the church in Corinth. This entire chapter concerns marriage, and the apostle begins by writing,

> Now concerning the things whereof ye wrote unto me..."
>
> (1 Cor 7:1)

We observe, therefore, that Paul is here responding to a letter he received from the church in Corinth. In God's eternal wisdom, the letter he received has been lost to history. Nor does Paul record for us what questions he is particularly answering. Consequently, the chapter before us represents only one side of a conversation. Anyone who has read a book that is a published response to another book, will immediately understand the handicap of not knowing the contents of the first. In the case before us, while this loss may seem unfortunate, we must accept God's sovereignty. Our need, then, is to respond with prayer, caution, and diligent study. And it should be kept in mind that the contents of this chapter might not flow so obviously as other portions of Scripture.

In this regard, a few preliminary observations about the entire chapter are of use. First, it may be observed that throughout this chapter Paul addresses certain groups of people specifically. In verse 2, he addresses "every man" and "every woman." In verse 3, he addresses "the husband" and "the wife." In verse 8, he addresses "unmarried and widows." In verse 10, he addresses, "the married." Later on, in verse 27, he addresses those that are "bound to a wife," and "those that are loosed from a wife." And finally, in the last two verses, he addresses widows.

A general examination of Paul's letters reveals that he frequently addresses different groups of people specifically. For example, Paul sometimes addresses servants, sometimes children, sometimes fathers, and sometimes wives. What is written to wives, does not apply to husbands. Likewise, what is written to children does not apply to fathers. As in those places, so here in this chapter, it is important not to confuse the text by directing it to some other than to whom it was meant.

A second observation of the chapter as a whole is that the Greek text [1] underlying this chapter is divided into three paragraphs. The paragraphs are significant, because each paragraph deals with a specific category of marriage. This paragraph structure, and their distinction based on who is being addressed is somewhat obscured in the English, but not entirely. As was pointed out above, the fact that Paul addresses particular groups of people is obvious. It is not beyond the grasp of normal study to discern that all of these specific groups readily fall into three broad categories, as distinguished by the three paragraphs. Thus, the first paragraph (1 Cor 7:1-7) deals with single people and those in need of elementary instructions about marriage. The second paragraph (1 Cor 7:8-24) deals with various conflicts that married people might experience, whether that be the death of a spouse, conflicts with a spouse, or having an unbelieving spouse. And the third paragraph (1 Cor 7:25-40) deals with some specific issues about re-marriage. It is seen from this that the chapter also successively addresses the three ways in which a person may be unmarried: single (vs 1-7), separated (vs 10-16), and widowed (vs 25-40).

With this in mind, let us consider what this interesting chapter of the Bible says about marriage, by examining the first paragraph:

> Now concerning the things whereof ye wrote unto me: it is
> good for a man not to touch a woman. Nevertheless, to avoid

---

1   The Text that I use, commonly called the "Textus Receptus," is officially titled the "Greek Text Underlying the English Authorised Version of 1611" printed by the Trinitarian Bible Society.

fornication, let every man have his own wife, and let every woman have her own husband. Let the husband render unto the wife due benevolence: and likewise also the wife unto the husband. The wife has not power of her own body, but the husband: and likewise also the husband hath not power of his own body, but the wife. Defraud ye not one the other, except it be with consent for a time, that ye may give yourself to fasting and prayer; and come together again, that Satan tempt you not for your incontinency. But I speak this by permission, and not of commandment. For I would that all men were even as I myself. But every man hath his proper gift of God, one after this manner, and another after that.

(1 Cor 7:1-7)

The apostle begins his response with a statement of fact: "it is good for a man not to touch a woman." The sentence is not a command, but a statement. So there may be times when a man might touch a woman. For instance, a man might help a woman up, as the apostle Peter did. (Acts 9:41). Likewise we read that a woman is commended for "washing the feet of the saints." (1 Tim 5:10). Nevertheless, this first sentence is still a statement of fact: "It is not good for a man to touch a woman." Therefore, we should not hide from this truth, nor from this word *touch*, as the New International Version (NIV) does. Sadly, the NIV paraphrases this first verse with the words: "It is good for a man not to marry." But in translating it thus, the NIV has overthrown the sense of this chapter, overthrown all of Scripture as it relates to marriage, and obliterated the importance of not touching a woman. Indeed, the true meaning is confirmed throughout the Scriptures, even by the account of godly Boaz, who said to Ruth, "I have charged the young men that they shall not touch thee." (Ruth 2:9).

In the second verse we read: "Let every man have his own wife, and let every woman have her own husband." Modern English somewhat obscures the force of these words, for the word *let* normally implies permission. Thus some might take this verse to mean: "Allow every man to have a wife." But this is not what is meant, for the Greek is an imperative command. The verse could have been translated, "Every man **must** have his own wife, and every woman **must** have her own husband." It is not my intent to fault the KJV here, for it is usual to translate Greek imperatives (of the third person: he/she) with the English words, "Let ...." The English has an imperative form only when speaking directly to someone. Thus, for example, we can say "Do this!" to either ourself, or to someone present. But how do we express a command to someone indirectly? It is usual to express it with the words: "Let them do this!" And indeed, this is how the KJV puts it: "Let every man have his own wife." It is an imperative command. Therefore, everyone, whether man or woman, should marry.

It is interesting that God has built the essence of this command into the very fabric of the two main languages of Scripture: Hebrew and Greek. The Greek word for woman (*gunaikos*) can mean either *woman* or *wife*. Likewise, the Greek word for man (*andros*) can mean either *man* or *husband*. It is similar with the Hebrew language. And here, then, by this command, and by the very nature of the language used to express it, we learn that God both wants and expects all people to marry.

Though the apostle commands every man and woman to marry, he does not here provide the least bit of instruction or counsel on how to find a spouse. Has the apostle forgotten so important a matter? How many hundreds of single Christians today wonder where they might find, 'God's Handbook to Finding a Spouse.' However, Paul's omission is of no significance, for it is obvious from this chapter that the Corinthians understood God's intent and wisdom. If there is a problem, it is entirely with ourselves and our unique culture of marriage and finding a spouse. As these things will be brought to light as we progress through this chapter, I pass them by for now, even as the apostle Paul did.

There is a reason given for this command, for the apostle wrote: "to avoid fornication, let every man have his own wife, and let every woman have her own husband." It is hard to see from this other than that all should marry young. Again, even the meaning of the Greek words for man/husband and woman/wife intimate this as well. Does a boy become a man? Then it is expected he will be a husband. Does a girl become a woman? Then it is expected she will be a wife. And does not the very reason given here for this command prove this? For the Holy Spirit has given us a reason, namely, "To avoid fornication." It were very strange indeed, to think that to avoid fornication one could marry much later on in life. So, then let every man and woman marry young.

The attentive reader will notice that the word, *avoid*, is italicized in the KJV, meaning that the word is not found in the Greek text. In fact, the Greek literally says, "on account of fornication, let every man...." Therefore, we learn from this reason, and by the fact that the command applies universally to all, that Christians are not super-naturally freed from sexual temptations. Nor are they transformed out of their bodies, but dwell in them as long as they live.

Dear reader, do these conclusions surprise you? Maybe you are one of those that have counselled young people that they should be content with being single, or that God might want them to remain single all their lives. Or maybe you have been one of those older believers that have advised youth that they need not worry about an early marriage, but should learn to control their minds. If it be so, you have sadly counselled contrary to the Scriptures, and placed the very young people you have tried to help in desperately dangerous positions.

Does this surprise the reader even more? Is the solution, maybe, that these commands are unique to the Corinthians? Or are these conclusions supported by other texts of Scripture? This last question is especially important, for many professing Christians in North America freely tell young singles that God might want them to remain single all their life. And rare indeed is it today to find any promoting young marriages. The text before us is adequately clear. But what does the rest of Scripture say?

Beginning at the beginning, we read: "And God blessed them and said, be fruitful and multiply, and fill the earth..." (Genesis 1:28). This is a command. While it was said specifically to Adam and Eve, it must be understood to equally apply to all their descendants, for without us helping, it were absurd to think that Adam and Eve could have enough children on their own to fill the earth. Indeed, the command is to "multiply." And multiplication can only happen when children also marry and bear children. Further, the command was repeated to Noah and his sons: "Be fruitful and multiply and fill the earth." (Gen 9:1). And it was again repeated to Jacob, and that after he had 12 sons already: "Be fruitful and multiply." (Gen 35:11). Here it is explicitly seen that the command to multiply is meant to apply to the children, for Jacob never had any more children after this command, at least none that are recorded. Therefore, by this three-fold repetition of the same command, and by the clearness with which it is meant to apply to their children, the command applies to us as equally.

Furthermore, the Scriptures give more specific instructions about each person's responsibility to marry. For instance, after God brought Adam his wife, He says, "Therefore shall a man leave his father and his mother and shall cleave unto his wife, and they shall be one flesh." (Gen 2:24). By this, God establishes a universal principle, applicable to all men - namely that they shall leave their parents to cleave unto a wife. That this statement is meant to be a universal principle for all men in particular is undeniable upon reflection of this text on its own, and given the context. But the matter is reinforced throughout all of Scripture, from one end to the other. I refer the reader to all the genealogies in the Scripture which say: 'And so and so begat so and so who begat so and so who begat so and so.' But never do we read, "And so and so felt he was content to be single." The generations continue, except for the occasional tragedy, such as, "but Seled died without children." (1 Chron 2:30). And without doubt, the Scriptures view this as a tragedy. Take, for instance, the fearful curse that fell on Agag: "As thy sword has made women childless, so shall thy mother be childless." (1 Sam 15:33) Hence, it is not particularly surprising that God gave instructions to His people on how to recover from such a tragedy, namely that the man's brother was to marry his widow and raise up children in his name - showing clearly that God intended all men both to marry and to have children. If it is such a curse or tragedy to be childless, how much greater of a curse and tragedy is it to never marry? Indeed, it is such a great tragedy that the Jews hold a yearly lamentation to commemorate one poor virgin that died before she could marry! (Jud 11:37-40).

We may also observe from this first text about marriage, that leaving home and getting married are considered one and the same event. Is a son ready to move out of the house? Then he is ready for marriage and should marry. Here again, it is seen that God expects people to marry young. Consider the particular example of the Babylonian captivity. The prophet Jeremiah wrote to the exiles, saying, "Take ye wives and beget sons and daughters, and take ye wives for your sons, and give your daughters to husbands, that they may bear... that ye may increase there and not diminish." (Jer 29:6). Here it is seen that even in the midst of terrible trials, of the desolation of the Jewish church, of the temporary abolishment of proper temple services, and when captive in a foreign land, the Jews were specifically commanded to marry and have children.

Someone might ask: Why then did God command Jeremiah not to marry? The reason which God gave to Jeremiah was that there were no godly women left in Jerusalem, and because death was so eminent. (Jer 16:1-6). Nevertheless, God was not so much forbidding Jeremiah from marrying, as forbidding him from remarrying after his first wife died. Earlier Jeremiah had himself complained, "Woe is me for my hurt! .... My tabernacle is spoiled... for my children are gone forth of me and they are not: there is none to stretch forth my tent anymore." (Jer 10:19,20). And as will be noted as we progress through our chapter in Paul's letter to the Corinthians, it is usual for God to advise widowers not to remarry. (1 Cor 7:8,27,40).

In another passage, we read: "Marriage is honourable in all." (Heb 13:4). And the clear meaning is that it is honourable for all to marry.

Nor is the Scripture lacking in places that teach that God expects all to marry young. The Psalmist writes, "Children are a heritage from the Lord... As arrows in the hand of a mighty man, so are children of the youth. Happy is the man that hath his quiver full of them." (Psa 127:3-5). It is impossible for a man to have many children of his youth unless he particularly marries young. In Proverbs, we read, "Let thy fountain be blessed, and rejoice with the wife of thy youth." (Pr 5:18). It is evident that the Holy Spirit takes for granted that all men that read Proverbs married when they were young.

In view of these things, it is no surprise that the Word of God should insist that one of the primary qualifications of a church leader is that he is "the husband of one wife." (1 Tim 3:2, Titus 1:6). Elders are of necessity older (this is what "elder" means), and therefore if they are "blameless," they will have followed God's instructions and married, even married young. Therefore, let us banish the unscriptural idea of a "celibate clergy." And let us likewise reject the idea that a single man qualifies to be an elder in the church, for God commands otherwise.

More Scriptures could be brought forth to prove that God wants all to marry, and that it is expected that all will marry young, but to be brief, I pass them by. What has been provided is surely sufficient.

Therefore, it is clear throughout the Scriptures, and from the particular command in Paul's first letter to the Corinthians, that God commands all men and women to marry. It is very tragic that this command has been ignored in the Western world. It is even claimed by Statistics Canada that for the first time more than half the Canadian population is not currently married.[2] Sadly, this severe problem is not restricted to unbelievers, but is common in churches too. How often do we hear of Christians that are single? Surely this testifies to a huge problem in the church - both in understanding the importance of marriage for all, but also in finding Biblical ways to obtain

---

2   Statistics Canada for 2007 is: Population: 32,976,026, Married: 15,916,860, Single: 13,800,997, Widowed: 1,573,455, and Divorced: 1,684,714. Less than half the population of Canada is legally married.

a spouse. Worse yet, the obvious effect of such appalling numbers of singles is exactly what the apostle here states, namely that fornication is rampant - both in the church and in the world.

But leaving this tragedy, let us return to our chapter now before us. After giving this instruction that all singles should marry, Paul immediately provides sound wisdom for those that are married. First of all, in the third verse, he commands both husband and wife to "render due benevolence" to each other. The Greek word translated here as *due,* means a debt is owed. And this is confirmed where Moses writes that if a man takes a wife, he must not deprive her of "her duty of marriage." (Ex 21:10). The next verse of our text in Corinthians provides somewhat of an explanation of this debt, saying, "The wife has not power of her own body, but the husband: and likewise also the husband hath not power of his own body, but the wife." (7:4). Here, in beautiful and respectful language, our Creator God delicately describes the human side of the "duty of marriage." Let the reader contemplate this verse, for it contains much truth.

Sadly, this truth is frequently rejected. Nor should such rejection surprise us, for the pride of man does not like to admit that another might have power over his body. But in the wisdom of God, this is how He has made us. And none that understand it aright can deny the wonder or beauty of it. We learn, then, that it is a universal matter of creation that God has given to the woman some power over the man's body, and to the man some power over the woman's body. The reality of these powers is no reflection of lack of spiritual victory, but of the way God made us. In marriage, it is beautiful and honourable. Outside of marriage, it is defrauding, and rapidly degrades into abominable sins.

Without delving too far into this mystery, and speaking only generally, we can learn from the Scriptures that at least part of the power that a man has over the woman's body is through touch. Hence our very chapter begins with the command: "It is good for a man not to touch a woman." (1 Cor 7:1). So then, it is especially important for men not to touch women, because of the way God has created us, and the inherit power given. Wicked men abuse this power, by using it to seduce women. (See: Deut 22:28, Ex 22:16).

We can also learn from the Scriptures that women, at least in part, have power over the man's body through sight. Thus, God speaks to Ezekiel about his wife, calling her "the desire of your eyes." (Ezek 24:16. See also: Jud 14:1, 16:1). Also, women are instructed to dress modestly, as it says, "I counsel, therefore.... that women adorn themselves in modest apparel, with shamefacedness, and sobriety." (1 Tim 2:9). That wicked women abuse this their power over men, the world is full of evidence from one end to the other. And the Scriptures contain so many texts and warnings that one would be wearied in documenting it. But that no one be left wondering, I refer to that which wise Solomon wrote, "And behold, there met him a woman with the attire of an harlot, and subtil of heart." (Pr 7:10). It is no strange thing that harlots dress a certain way. So then, it is especially important for women to dress modestly, lest they abuse their power over the man's body.

We learn from these things that most modern styles of dance are forbidden by God, for not only do most kinds of dance require men to touch women, but women are encouraged in them to dress immodestly. And it is immediately discerned from this why dancing is so poplar, for it feeds the powers of the one over the other. But let the careful reader discern that all the proper dancing recorded in the Bible was either on one's own, as when David danced before the Lord, or with the genders separated, as when Miriam went out and danced with the women. (Ex 15:20).

Dear reader, we see from these things how far modern churches have strayed from Biblical truth, for single men are rarely discouraged from touching women, and single women are frequently running with earnest, not to clothe themselves modestly, but to clothe themselves in sexy garments. What can be said of this? It is surely a huge disgrace to the Christian church. And it is no wonder that, as the text before us explicitly informs us, the result is that the sins of fornication and adultery abound in the church.

Nevertheless, God's word here stands for all that have ears to hear, condemning all such defrauding behaviour, and encouraging us to overcome with good by honourable marriage, and honour in marriage.

In the fifth verse, the apostle again confirms the debt of benevolence, saying, "Defraud ye not one the other, except it be with consent for a time, that ye may give yourself to fasting and prayer; and come together again, that Satan tempt you not for your incontinency." (7:5) Thus, periods of abstinence are permitted within the marriage, but only with mutual consent, and then only for a time. The reader will observe that mutual consent is a requirement for abstinence, not for union. In the preceding verse, the word translated as *power* can equally be translated as *authority*. Thus, in the matter of the duty of marriage, the wife has authority over the husband's body, and the husband has authority over the wife's body. And while some might cavil at such a teaching, these verses beautifully demonstrate the fullness to which God has made the husband and wife one flesh. Marriage is not two people co-habiting, but one new person.

It is taken for granted that the purpose for such times of abstinence is entirely spiritual - to pray and fast. We also see again the delicate state of our humanity, for even in marriage it is possible for couples to defraud each other. And, it is easy for Satan to tempt couples if such times of abstinence are unnecessarily long.

In harmony with this instruction is the sad fact that the adulterous woman that Solomon warns against had become accustomed to her husband being absent for extended periods. Indeed, in trying to seduce her neighbour, she says: "The goodman is not at home, he is gone a long journey: he hath taken a bag of money with him, and will come home at the day appointed." (Pr 7:19,20). Nevertheless, her husband's error is no excuse for her sin. She remains an adulteress, and "her house is the way to hell." (Pr 7:27).

The apostle follows these instructions by saying, "But I speak this by permission, and not of commandment. For I would that all men were even as I myself. But every man hath his proper gift of God, one after this manner, and another after that." (7:6,7) This is an interesting text, and prone to confusion. Some claim by this that Paul was a single man, that he is speaking of a gift of celibacy, and that he hereby grants permission for some to remain single. This was the interpretation of the Roman Catholic church of the Middle Ages, and it led to the innumerable accounts of fornication among monks and nuns. It may be refuted by careful consideration of the text. First, Paul was not a single man, but a widower, as may be seen from verse 8, and which will be shown more fully below. Second, it would be highly unusual for Paul to have meant the words, "I speak this" to refer to anything other than the preceding sentence, for that is usual. Third, it has already been shown that the Scriptures teach that all singles should marry. And fourth, it is impossible that Paul should wish all men to be single - as that would be the end of both church and humanity in but one generation.

Therefore, the words, "I speak this by permission," refers to the times of voluntary abstinence. From this we learn that all are not equally empowered with self-restraint. Indeed, Paul confirms this even more clearly a few verses later, for when addressing widows and widowers he advises that some should marry, and some might wish to remain unmarried. Therefore, these comments about abstinence in marriage are optional: some might not wish to abstain at all, even for fasting and prayer, while others might wish to abstain for a longer period of time. Whatever the case, it remains that it must be by mutual "consent."

The fact that the apostle refers to this matter with the words, "every man hath his proper gift of God," teaches us of the Sovereignty of God in all of His creation. All are not created the same when it comes to these matters of defrauding and temptation. Some are tempted very strongly, others hardly at all. Let each accept the way that God has made him. And let each learn to be discreet so as not to offend his brother. We may also see more clearly why the Scriptures so frequently refer to lewdness and obscene clothing in such derogatory terms, why woman are commanded to dress modestly, and why men should not touch women. If married people may be tempted by even a short period of abstinence, what must be the case of young singles? Indeed, the very text before us began by saying, "to avoid fornication, let every man have his own wife, and let every woman have her own husband."

This ends the apostle's discourse towards young singles, and those first married. Let us turn now to the second paragraph of our chapter.

CHAPTER 2

Challenges in Marriage: Death of a Spouse, Marital Conflicts

We come now to the second paragraph of our chapter, in which the apostle deals with various challenging circumstances that married people might find themselves in. The text particularly addresses the subjects of widows and widowers (vs 8,9), divorce and separation (vs 10,11), and an unbelieving spouse (vs 12-16). The last part of this second paragraph is mostly an aside in which the apostle provides insights into God's providence (vs 17-24). So then, the paragraph begins:

> I say therefore to the unmarried and widows, it is good for them
> if they abide even as I. But if they cannot contain, let them marry:
> for it is better to marry than to burn.
>
> (1 Cor 7:8,9)

Here Paul specifically addresses the unmarried (masculine plural) and widows (feminine plural). The English word *unmarried* can refer to those that have never married, those that are separated/divorced, or those that are widowed. It was earlier noted that each of these three is addressed in a separate paragraph in this chapter. Those that have never married are addressed in the first paragraph, those that are separated in this second paragraph, and the widowed primarily in the third paragraph.

But it is useful to note that the Greek word translated here as *unmarried* is not so broad as the English word. The word which was here translated as *unmarried* is not found any where in the Bible, except in this chapter. And here in this chapter, even in the English language, it is not that difficult to conclude that the word *unmarried* always refers to those that were married. Thus, for example, in verse 8, Paul is speaking to widowers (masculine plural) and widows (feminine plural). In verse 11, Paul speaks of the woman that is unmarried because she is separated from her husband, saying, "let her remain unmarried." In verses 32 and 33, Paul contrasts the unmarried man with the married man - but he is speaking to those that are "bound to a wife" and those that were "loosed from a wife." Therefore by *unmarried* he means someone "loosed from a wife," not someone that never married. But the strongest proof is that in the first paragraph, which is particularly addressed to singles that have never married, Paul does not use the term *unmarried*. Therefore, it is observed that the word *unmarried* as used in this chapter only applies to people that were once married. That is, it may refer to widows, widowers, divorced or to those that are separated. But the person that never married is excluded from this term.

This conclusion is reinforced by a closer consideration of the Greek word that is here translated as *unmarried*. In the Greek language, there are three words for women: there is a word for a virgin (*parthenos*), one for a woman/wife (*gunaika*), and one for a widow (chera). But for the man, there is essentially only one word: a man/husband (*andros*). To the best of my knowledge, there is no Greek word, either for a young man that has never married, nor for a widower. This would explain why the apostle, in verse 8, addressed the "unmarried and widows" instead of "widowers and widows," namely that there is no Greek word for *widower*. But his meaning is clear. And the Corinthians would certainly have understood him this way. Further, the word here translated *unmarried* is the word, *agamos*. In the Greek language, an "a" (α pronounced alpha) is placed in front of a noun to negate it. It is similar to the way English uses the prefix "un-" to denote negation. Thus, *un-married* means not married; *unhappy* means not happy. However, the Greek prefix, alpha, properly "denotes privation" (Moulton). And the word *privation* contains more than simple negation; it more precisely means, "The state of being deprived, or the act of removing something possessed" (Webster). Since the Greek word, *gamos* means married, the word, *agamos* properly means deprived of marriage, or no longer married. Thus, in verse 11, speaking to a separated woman, Paul says, "let her remain unmarried." Clearly, the meaning is that the woman had in some sense been deprived of her married state, not that she was never married.

It is clear from other Greek words (ie. pistos and apistos: faithful and unfaithful) that the alpha prefix does not always denote privation, but sometimes only means the negative, as the simple English prefix, "un-" does. Nevertheless, there is no reason why *agamos* should not be taken as having a proper meaning; and the context supports this conclusion. Therefore, here in verse 8, Paul is addressing widowers and widows.

We learn from this, then, that however good and pleasant marriage is, it does not last into eternity. Sadly, usually one spouse dies before the other, leaving the other to grieve the loss. And by this we are again brought to see the humble state in which mankind lives. Our bodies are fragile; our lives are short. Indeed, a few verses later, the apostle reminds us of this, saying, "Brethren, the time is short: it remaineth, that both they that have wives be as though they had none, and they that weep [at the loss of their spouse] as though they wept not, and they that rejoice [in their new spouse] as though they rejoiced not... For the fashion of this world passeth away." (7:29,31). And we are again reminded of the Sovereignty of God, who alone determines which spouse will die first, as it says, "It is appointed unto men once to die." (Heb 9:27).

What advice does Paul offer those that have lost a spouse? He writes, "It is good for them if they abide even as I." And here it is seen that Paul was a widower. The fact that this is prone to surprise many Christians today only proves the sad fact that we have deluded ourselves to the point where we expect some people to be single. Paul was a Jew. And further, he was a Pharisee. It is virtually incomprehensible that such should be single. For as was pointed out above, the Old Testament Scriptures everywhere promote marriage, bearing children, and multiplying. Indeed, the Bible teaches that just to have a wife is a particular blessing from God (Pr 18:22). Would it be possible for one like Paul, who was zealous for the traditions of his fathers with a zeal that surpassed all his contemporaries, not to have eagerly participated in an early marriage? It is impossible. But speculation is not needed, for Paul here specifically puts himself in the camp of the widower.

Therefore, Paul is advising those that have lost a spouse that it is good if they stay unmarried. The same advice is given in the third paragraph, in which Paul deals with certain issues of remarriage. There we read, "Art thou loosed from a wife? Seek not a wife." (7:27). And again, later on, he says to the widow "she is happier if she so abide." (7:40). But lest there be any confusion, the apostle makes it very clear that this is not a rigid command of God. Indeed, the apostle immediately points out that not all are able to remain unmarried. Such are told: "If they cannot contain, let them marry, for it is better to marry than to burn." And later on he writes, "but and if thou marry, thou hast not sinned." (7:28). And finally, he adds that the widow "is at liberty to be married to whom she will; only in the Lord." (vs 39). Three times Paul gives his opinion that the widowed not remarry, and three times he tells them it is not sin if they do.

How does this advice compare to other Scriptures? Concerning Biblical histories, we read of the men of Israel finding new wives for the men of Benjamin that had lost their first wives in war. (Jud 21) And we read of Naomi desiring to find new husbands for her widowed daughters-in-law. (Ruth 1). We read that king David married a widow (1 Sam 25:39). Further, Abraham married again after Sarah died. (Gen 25:1). All of this concurs with the fact that it is not sin for a widow or widower to remarry. And it informs us that many such in fact do remarry.

Yet we never read of Naomi finding a second husband for herself. And we do read that some widows in Israel returned to live with their fathers again. (Lev 22:13). Moreover, we know that Anna was a very old widow, and that she spent her days in fasting and prayer. (Lk 2:36,37). And we read that God commanded Jeremiah not to remarry. (Jer 16:2). All of this concurs with the fact that some widows and widowers remain unmarried.

It is very interesting, even strange at first, to consider what the same apostle wrote about widows in his letter to Timothy. In fact, the instructions appear to be the opposite, for there Paul writes: "I counsel therefore that the younger women marry, bear children, guide the house, give none occasion to the adversary to speak reproachfully." (1 Tim 5:14). And by "younger women," Paul expressly means widows under 60 years of age (1 Tim 5:9). The question begs to be asked: Why would Paul advise the Corinthians that it is best for widows not to remarry, but then tell Timothy that widows should remarry? Is Paul contradicting himself here?

We should not wish to accuse Paul, nor the Holy Spirit who inspired him, of being double-tongued. The answer to this question is that in his letter to Timothy, Paul distinguishes between older and younger widows: the younger widows are taught to remarry; but nothing particular is said to the older widows. In fact, it is taken for granted that all the older widows will remain unmarried. Further, it is observable that part of the reason Paul addressed the issue is that the younger widows were trying to remain unmarried - only to fall into trouble. It is very likely, then, that by the time Paul wrote his letter to Timothy, his counsel to the Corinthians had taken firm root in the churches. The letter to the Corinthians, however, makes no distinction between older widows and younger ones. Indeed, it is clear from the way that Paul systematically addresses the various groups of people in this chapter that he is dealing in broad generalities - speaking to singles, the married, and widows. In general, God appoints 70 or 80 years of life, as the Bible says (Psa 90:10). Therefore, in the normal course of life, a married man or woman might lose a spouse after they are 60 years of age. Paul's advice to the Corinthians is under the assumption that the widow or widower is somewhat advanced in age. But if they are younger, then the instructions to Timothy apply, and they should re-marry. The fact that younger widows are instructed to remarry is all the more proof that all singles should marry, and that they should marry young.

After addressing the challenge of the death of a spouse, Paul turns to address a second challenge that married couples might experience, saying,

> And unto the married I command, yet not I, but the Lord, Let not the wife depart from her husband: but and if she depart, let her remain unmarried, or be reconciled to her husband: and let not the husband put away his wife.
>
> (1 Cor 7:10,11)

Here the apostle deals with the reality of marital strife. While marriage is honourable, and while it is normal and expected for the "bridegroom to rejoice over the bride," (Isa 62:5), yet the sad reality is that there is still the possibility of conflict in marriage - even among Christians. The apostle does not here stop to give any counsel about how to either avoid or solve marriage conflicts. Therefore, following the same course, I leave such matters to other authors and other texts of Scripture. After all, it is certain that the Bible contains divine wisdom on solving all human conflicts, not just marital ones. Indeed, the very letter containing this chapter addresses many conflicts, and provides useful instruction on how Christians should deal with them.

But though Paul gives no counsel here on resolving conflicts, he is very bold to tell us that divorce is not an option for Christians. The reader is again reminded that the English word, "Let...." when used as it is here, is the usual way to translate an imperative command in the Greek. Therefore, the words, "Let not the wife depart from her husband," is a command; a prohibition. The wife must not depart from her husband. And the husband must not put away his wife. And Paul is very bold to affirm that these are commands of God.

Only one exception is granted here, and that to the wife, namely that "if she depart, let her remain unmarried or be reconciled to her husband." I presume that this exception is allowed as a kindness to the woman because she is the "weaker vessel." (1 Peter 3:7). Indeed, in the very text that describes women as the weaker vessels, men are encouraged "to dwell with their wife in knowledge, giving honour unto them." We learn from this the sad reality that even amongst Christians couples, there may be times when the marriage is so stressed, that the wife feels she has no other recourse than to leave for a time. But it will be noted that Paul gives no such exception for the man. He is not allowed to put away his wife - not for any reason. Nor is he permitted to depart himself.

Therefore, let us learn to be very tender towards Christian couples that are struggling in their marriages. Let us not cast them off as unbelievers, for this Paul does not do. Rather, let us pray for them, and strive to help them delicately. And let us encourage them to stay together.

We learn also from this, that if a woman leaves a man, she has only two options: either remain unmarried, or be reconciled to her husband. This abundantly testifies to the fact that divorce is of the devil, and that divorce and remarriage is completely unscriptural.

As many professing Christians may be surprised at these strong words, it is worthwhile to investigate the matter more thoroughly. As the matter is weighty, and since there are so many texts that apply, the matter has been placed in a chapter of its own.

CHAPTER 3

The Christian View of Divorce

It was seen in the previous chapter that divorce is not an option for the believer. As this matter is almost universally challenged among modern churches, and since it is so fundamental an issue, it is certainly worthwhile to investigate the Scriptures further. Are Paul's instructions to the Corinthians unique? Or, do the rest of the Scriptures concur?

In this chapter, the matter will be investigated by examining the entire Bible, first by considering the Law of God in the books of Moses, next, what the Prophets of God in the Old Testament wrote, third, what our Lord Jesus Himself said during His earthly ministry, and finally, we will consider what the apostles wrote in their New Testament letters.

1. What the Law of God says about Marriage and Divorce

First, then, what does the Law of God say about divorce and marriage? What did Moses write? The Law has much to say about this matter. I begin with the commandment: "Thou shalt not commit adultery." (Ex 20:14). It is of particular interest to note that this commandment is, very strangely, not in the imperative tense. It does not say: "Thou must not commit adultery." Rather, it is written in the future tense. (Today you are here, tomorrow *you shall* be there.) The verse could equally have been translated, "You will not commit adultery," or, "You are not going to commit adultery." It is more of a prophecy about the future, than a command for the present. We learn from this, therefore, that God fully expects, and thus empowers, His people not to commit adultery.

Another law says, "Thou shalt not lie carnally with thy neighbor's wife to defile thyself with her." (Lev 18:20). The word *wife* is more broad and encompassing than the way we currently use the word. Thus, for instance, a woman pledged to be married is given the significant status of wife: "If a damsel that is a virgin be betrothed unto an husband, and a man find her in the city, and lie with her; then shall ... ye stone them... that they die; the damsel because she cried not, being in the city, and the man, because he hath humbled his neighbour's wife." (Deut 22:23,24). Observe that although the woman was a virgin, she is considered a wife because betrothed. In like manner, Joseph and Mary are called by God in the Scriptures as husband and wife, even before they were married. (Mt 1:19).

This law about the betrothed virgin is in stark contrast to the law a few verses later: "If a man find a damsel that is a virgin, which is not betrothed, and lay hold on her, and lie with her, and they be found: then.... she shall be his wife, for he has humbled her, he may not put her away all his days." (Deut 22:28,29). Thus a woman pledged to be married had a status significantly different from a virgin not so pledged. And it is also to be observed that the man in this last text is forbidden from divorcing his wife. Thus God through Moses begins the doctrine that divorce is non-optional.

Let us now consider more particularly the teaching about divorce. In the Law, if a man accused his wife of not having been a virgin when he married her, (i.e. she was unfaithful before they were married), but she is found to be innocent, God says: "She shall be his wife; he may not put her away all his days." (Deut 22:13-21). It is seen from this text, that if a man marries a virgin he is never allowed to divorce her. And, as was noted above, this is true even if the marriage came about after a man seduced a virgin. Therefore, the only acceptable cause for a divorce is unfaithfulness before the marriage.

Indeed, the Law forbade a man from marrying a woman who had fornicated, for such was considered a prostitute by God in the Law. In the second text above (Deut 22:13-19), if a man discovered that his wife had been unfaithful before marriage, she was to be put to death, "because she hath wrought folly in Israel, to play the whore in her father's house: so shalt thou put evil away from among you." (Deut 22:21). Likewise, the Levites, as examples of righteousness in the land, were commanded: "They shall not take a wife that is a whore, or profane, neither shall they take a woman put away from her husband, for he (the Levite) is holy unto his God." (Lev 21:7). It is for this reason that Joseph, the husband of Mary, was commended by God as a righteous man, for when he discovered that his betrothed wife was pregnant, he intended to divorce her as the law commanded. (Mt 1:18-20).

Nevertheless, God, knowing the weakness of mankind and our proneness to all manner of strife and conflict, did not fail to acknowledge the reality of divorce and separation within the Israelite society. Thus, for example, Moses writes that if a husband had two wives but did not provide one with food, clothing and marital rights, she was permitted to leave him. (See Ex 21:10,11. See also Deut 21:10-14). But as in our text in First Corinthians, the woman was not given permission to remarry. And no freedom is given to the man to leave his wife. A second example to illustrate how God acknowledged the reality of divorce regards vows. The Law states: "But every vow of a widow, and of her that is divorced... shall stand against her." (Num 30:9). Here again, it is taken for granted that the divorced woman remains unmarried, for had she remarried, then her vow would only stand if her husband permitted it.

Though God acknowledged the reality of divorce and separation, never does He approve of it, and He certainly condemns remarriage. Thus, the Priests, as the teachers of righteousness in Israel, were expressly forbidden from marrying a divorced woman: "They shall not take a wife... that is put away from her husband, for he is holy unto his God." (Lev 21:7). Indeed, divorced women were cared for by God only if they never remarried. "If a priest's daughter be a widow or divorced, and have no child, and is returned unto her father's house, as in her youth, she shall eat of her father's meat." (Lev 22:13). In this text, the "father's meat" refers to the sacred food given to the priests by the Lord. And no unauthorized persons could eat of it. Nevertheless, in spite of its sacred nature and such strong warnings, God allowed divorced women to eat of it as long as they remained unmarried (i.e. they lived in their father's house again.). By all of this we see a beautiful picture of God's righteous will, for it tells us that God promises to look after and care for a divorced woman, just as He would a widow, as long as she remains unmarried.

Finally, let us consider the law that specifically concerns divorce and remarriage. This law is the law that the Pharisees mentioned to Jesus when they were trying to test Him. The law says:

> When a man hath taken a wife, and married her, and it come to pass that she find no favour in his eyes, because he hath found some uncleanness in her; then let him write her a bill of divorcement,

and give it in her hand, and send her out of his house. And when she is departed out of his house, she may go and be another man's wife. And if the latter husband hate her; and write her a bill of divorcement, and giveth it in her hand, and sendeth her out of his house; or if the latter husband die, which took her to be his wife; her former husband, which sent her away, may not take her again to be his wife, after that she is defiled; for that is abomination before the Lord; and thou shalt not cause the land to sin..."

(Deut 24:1-4).

Although we are presently considering what the Law says about marriage and divorce, yet since Christ addressed this particular law, it is instructive for us to consider His words. Jesus said: "Moses because of the hardness of your hearts suffered you to put away your wives, but from the beginning it was not so." (Mt 19:8). It will be further observed that when Christ said these words, He was answering the question, "Why did Moses command to give a writing of divorcement?" (Mt 19:7). Jesus wisely shifts the question, pointing out that this law was not a **command** to divorce, but **permission** to do so.

What, then, is the primary intent of this law? Is it to give directions on how to go about a divorce? No - though some information about this is provided. Is it to give valid causes for a divorce? No, though one cause is mentioned. Is it to give permission for a woman to remarry after being divorced? Not at all, though it assumes she will. What then is this law about? It is a law regarding whether or not a divorced woman that had remarried could return to her first husband. This, says God, is detestable. It is a great sin. Though God hates divorce, and though adultery is terrible, this thing of returning to one's first husband after a second marriage ended, (whether it ended by divorce or death), is identified here with the worst of all terms: abomination. That is the point of this law.

But since mention is made here of other things, we might learn from them. Observe, first of all, that the cause for the first divorce is that the man finds "some uncleanness" in his wife. In other words, marital unfaithfulness is the only cause for a divorce, as has already been pointed out above. But it is observed that so far the Law has only made mention of unfaithfulness before the wedding takes place. Here, however, it is noted that the woman was already living in the man's house, for the text says that he sent "her from his house." In the case of unfaithfulness before the marriage, a man is commanded to put his wife away. But in the case of unfaithfulness after marriage, a man is only "permitted" to put his wife away, and this only because his heart might be hard. Indeed, it is the hardness of a man's heart that prevents him from loving his wife after she sins.

And let us consider where it says, "she may go and be another man's wife." (Deut 24:2b). Does this word, *may*, give the woman permission to remarry? Although *may* can refer to permission, the word can also mean, if perhaps. For example, one might say, "You may be sick tomorrow." This is not a statement of permission or ability, but of possibility. It is the context that determines the meaning. And it should be clear from the text that this law concerns a hypothetical situation. This is certain from the times the word *if* is used. Therefore, we should interpret the word *may* as a statement of possibility, not of permission. In other words, it is possible (even highly likely) that a woman that is divorced because of her unfaithfulness, will marry another man. Jesus is even more clear on this, but I pass that by until we come to His words more particularly.

It is also to be noted that Moses takes for granted that the first husband remains unmarried, for when the woman leaves the second marriage, the first husband is in a position where he might "take her again to be his wife." And this is the case even though the man divorced his wife because there was something unclean about her.

In summary then, the Law of God teaches that marriage is for life. Divorce is forbidden under all circumstances except when a spouse has been unfaithful. If the unfaithfulness occurs before the wedding, then divorce is demanded. If it occurs after the wedding, a divorce is permitted, but not recommended. But God forbids such a divorced person from remarrying.

It will be observed that this is precisely what Paul has written to the Corinthians in the letter under consideration. Nor should this surprise us, for the New Testament teaches, "Do we then make void the law of God through faith? God forbid; yea, we establish the law." (Rom 3:31). Again, it says, "Is the law sin? God forbid. Nay, I had not known sin, but by the law." (Rom 7:7). And again, "I delight in the Law of God after the inward man." (Rom 7:22). And again, "We know that the law is good if a man use it lawfully." (1 Tim 1:8) And again, "This is love for God, when we keep his commandments." (1 John 5:3). And again, in the very chapter of our text, "Circumcision is nothing and uncircumcision is nothing, but the keeping of the commandments of God." (1 Cor 7:19)

2. The Prophets on Marriage and Divorce

Having considered what the Law says about divorce and remarriage, let us turn, secondly, to consider what the prophets say about this matter. So ingrained is the idea of singleness in our day, that frequently people think most of the prophets of God were single. Is it true? It is outright false. Moses was a prophet, and he had a wife and two sons. The prophet Samuel, who is called the first of the prophets (Acts 3:24), was married, for he had several sons (1 Sam 8:1). In the Scriptures we find frequent mention of groups of prophets from the days of Samuel and thereafter, suggesting that schools had been established for them in Israel. And it is instructive to note that we also read of the "sons of the prophets." (2 king 2:3). Therefore prophets had wives. Likewise, Isaiah had a wife that was prophetess, and she bore several sons to him. (Isa 7:3, 8:3). Jeremiah, as was already pointed out, had several children by his wife before she died. Ezekiel had a wife, as did Hosea. Therefore, from all these clear examples, it is rather to be assumed that all the prophets had wives and children. Indeed, nothing stands to the contrary.

Having therefore concluded that the prophets, by their own godly examples, endorse both marriage and having children, let us now consider what they, under the inspiration of the Holy Spirit, have said concerning divorce and remarriage.

The prophet Jeremiah writes, "If a man put away his wife, and she go from him, and become another man's, shall he return unto her again? Shall not the land be greatly polluted?" (Jer 3:1). Here the prophet confirms and reinforces the law of God as found in Deuteronomy 24, and which we discussed above. Yet is not this great pollution practised by some in our day? Have not some churches rejoiced to "re-unite" a divorced couple - though they had been married to others? And do not some insist that if a man repent of remarrying after a divorce, he must prove his repentance by divorcing his second wife and returning to his first? But God is not slow to inform us that such is a great abomination, and that it pollutes not only us but the land. Let us flee from such evidence of despising the word of God.

Can we flee? Is there room for repentance after the church has so horribly departed from God? Though a woman may not return to her husband if she has been married to another, yet God urges us to return to Him in spite of our wickedness. Indeed, this is the very point of Jeremiah's words, for the text proceeds to say, "But thou hast played the harlot with many lovers; yet return again to me, saith the Lord." (Jer 3:1b). Then let us return to so great and merciful a God, for He receives back abominable sinners!

But the Israelites had not only sinned by spiritual harlotry; indeed, Jeremiah goes on in his book to describe their outward sins, saying, "The land is full of adulterers." (Jer 23:10). And a few verses later he adds,

> "I have seen also in the prophets of Jerusalem an horrible thing: They commit adultery and walk in lies; they strengthen also the hands of evildoers, that none doth return from his wickedness. They are all of them unto me as Sodom...."
>
> (Jer 23:14)

Here we see that the problems facing the churches in North America are not so new as one might be inclined to think - for in Jeremiah's day, even the prophets of Jerusalem were committing adultery. But let us not be like those in our day that pass this by lightly, or like those in Jeremiah's day that strengthened people in their evil deeds. But let us be like Jeremiah, who grieved deeply at this wickedness among his brethren. Let us be willing to boldly call sin sin, and not cloak adultery under other names. Rather, let us encourage Christians to marry, to stay married, to refuse divorce, and to categorically refuse to marry a divorced person.

Turning from the prophet Jeremiah to Ezekiel, we discover that this prophet writes concerning priests, saying,

> "Neither shall they take for their wives a widow, nor her that is put away; but they shall take maidens of the seed of the house of Israel, or a widow that had a priest before. And they shall teach my people the difference between the holy and the profane, and cause them to discern between the unclean and the clean."
>
> (Ezek 44:22,23).

This text agrees with the law we examined for priests, as found in Leviticus 21:7, namely that priests were expressly forbidden from marrying divorced women. The reason given in both the Law and here by Ezekiel is that the priests were teachers in Israel and were to instruct the populace even by their actions in marriage. In that they were to marry "maidens," it is affirmed that one should not marry a woman that has fornicated in her youth. (See Deut 22:14). Various suggestions have been put forward concerning the restriction that a Levite might only marry a widow if she had previously been married to a priest. Whatever the case, it must be understood in the context that the priests were to set an example for all Israel. I conclude, therefore, that the restriction is placed primarily to prevent inheritance rights from passing from one tribe to another: for a widow possessed the property of her husband; and inheritances were not to pass between the tribes. (See Num 36:1-7, and Compare Ruth 3:1, 3:9, with 4:3).

Turning from Ezekiel, let us consider the prophet Hosea. This man of God had the difficult task of marrying an unfaithful woman, for God had commanded him saying, "Go take unto thee a wife of whoredoms and children of whoredoms, for the land hath committed great whoredoms in departing from the Lord." (Hos 1:2). Some are inclined to think that this woman had been unfaithful before Hosea married her. I sincerely doubt it, since the Scriptures expressly forbid marrying an unfaithful woman. Also, there is no particular mention of it in Hosea. God, who knows the future, could call her a "wife of whoredoms" before she committed any sin, even as Christ called Judas a traitor before he actually betrayed Him. (Lk 21:21, Jn 6:70,71). Rather, and as the context clearly reveals, Hosea's wife became an adulteress after bearing him several children. What was Hosea's response to this unfaithfulness? It was not left up for him to choose, for God specifically instructed him, saying, "Go yet, love a woman beloved of her friend, yet an adulteress, according to the love of the Lord toward the children of Israel...." (Hos 3:1).

It has been seen in the Law that Moses did not command divorce in such cases, but permitted it because of the hardness of men's hearts. Hosea, as a prophet and example of the love of God, was to love his poor wife, even in the face of her unfaithfulness. It will further be noted that there is a distinction between separation and divorce. If a man divorces his wife and she marries another, she is absolutely forbidden from coming back to him. However, if a wife is unfaithful while married, she is permitted to repent and return to her husband. The husband is permitted, if his heart is not too hard, to receive her back to himself. Hosea never divorced his wife. Nor did she marry another. She had departed from him and had committed adultery with her friend. Strictly speaking, the Law did not forbid Hosea from receiving his wife back.

It is observed, therefore, that both Jeremiah and Hosea were commanded by God to do something which is only recommended to others. Paul only advises widowers to remain unmarried; but Jeremiah is commanded not to remarry. The law only permits men to divorce their wife for unfaithfulness; but Hosea is commanded not to divorce her. And we learn from this the consistency of godly wisdom, whether in the Law, or the Prophets, or the apostles. We also learn that godly wisdom runs contrary to the flesh, and that the hardness of men's hearts hinder them from walking in the love of God.

Finally, let us turn from Hosea to Malachi, the last prophet before Christ came. And what does God say by this prophet? "For the Lord, the God of Israel, saith that he hateth putting away." (Mal 2:16). In other words, God hates divorce.

It is particularly useful to consider the context of this statement. Malachi, who wrote during the lifetime of Ezra and Nehemiah, had just addressed mixed marriages: "Judah hath profaned the holiness of the Lord, which he loved, and hath married the daughter of a strange god." (Mal 2:11). Indeed, both Ezra and Nehemiah own the extent of this tragedy, for many Israelites that had returned from Babylon had married non-Jewish women. (Ezra 9:1,2, and Neh 13:23-25). But Malachi, speaking the word of God, directs the people to a very different course of action than Ezra did. Sadly, Ezra listened to a friend, (Ezr 10:2), rather than the word of God or the prophet Malachi. And contrary to God's law, he concluded that the way to deal with the matter was to issue certificates of divorce, and to send away all the foreign women. (Ezr 9:3, 10:3). Malachi strongly rebukes the people for heeding the advice of Ezra, though without mentioning Ezra's name. And the prophet boldly declares that God did not care for all their tears, nor their violence against the offenders. Why? "Because the Lord hath been witness between thee and the wife of thy youth, against whom thou hast dealt treacherously: yet is she thy companion, and the wife of thy covenant. And did not He make them one?" (Mal 2:14-15). Therefore, once a marriage is consummated, God has made the two people one. And it does not matter that one spouse is an unbeliever. God hates divorce.

In conclusion, then, the prophets teach that marriage is commended and divorce is forbidden, even if one's spouse is an unbeliever. In the case of an unfaithful wife, divorce is permitted, but not recommended. It is observed, therefore, that the prophets taught identically to what Moses wrote in the Law of God. And this should certainly surprise no one, for the prophets, speaking by the Spirit of God, would certainly not contradict God's holy Law.

3. What Jesus Christ taught concerning Marriage and Divorce

Thirdly, then, let us consider what our Lord Jesus Christ said about divorce during His earthly ministry. In Luke's Gospel, we read that Christ said: "Whosoever putteth away his wife, and marrieth another, committeth adultery, and whosoever marrieth her that is put away from her husband committeth adultery." (Lk 16:18). It is observable that both these statements are made from the perspective of the man. If a man puts away his wife and remarries, he commits adultery. If a man marries a divorced woman, he commits adultery. It is further observed that the issue of adultery does not depend on who puts who away. For in the first case, the man put his wife away and yet is guilty of adultery if he remarries. And in the second case, though the woman was put away, the man that marries her commits adultery. It is also to be noted that the statements are made unconditionally, "Whosoever... and whosoever..." And finally, it is observed that Christ is not commenting here on divorce, but on remarriage, for in both statements it is in remarriage that the sin of adultery is committed. Therefore, whether one puts away, or is put away, no matter what the cause, to remarry is to commit adultery. It is useful to keep this general summary in mind when considering the other things which Christ says.

But before passing on to His other words, let us consider the context of this first statement. It is surely significant that Jesus had just said: "It is easier for heaven and earth to pass than one tittle of the Law to fail." (Lk 16:17). So then, if heaven and earth must pass away before one small stroke of the law does, it is certain that divorce will not annul the law of marriage. Therefore remarriage after a divorce is always adultery.

Matthew's Gospel records an occasion when Christ said something quite similar to this which Luke recorded. Here Jesus says,

> It has been said, 'Whosoever shall put away his wife, let him give her a writing of divorcement.' But I say unto you, that whosoever shall put away his wife, saving for the cause of fornication, causeth her to commit adultery; and whosoever shall marry her that is divorced committeth adultery.
>
> (Mt 5:31,32).

It is observed that in Luke's Gospel, Christ was particularly addressing the issue of remarriage, but in this text Jesus addresses both divorce and remarriage. And it is evident from these words that the Jews were taking far more liberties from the Law than God ever intended. Their words, "Whosoever shall put away his wife...." implies that they thought anyone can, for any cause. But Moses never gave such freedoms, as has already been shown above.

Our Lord corrects the people's mistaken use of the Law, by affirming what the Law actually taught, namely that there is only one acceptable cause for a divorce, which is fornication (unfaithfulness before marriage). And Christ also affirms that remarriage is the sin of adultery.

It is interesting to observe that Jesus says that when a man divorces his wife he "causes her to commit adultery." Our Lord did not say, "he causes himself to commit adultery," but that he causes his **wife** to do so. In other words, a divorce for unjust reasons is so wicked that it makes the other spouse, the wife in this case, commit adultery. It will be recalled from the Law (Deut 24) that Moses takes for granted that a divorced woman will remarry. Here it is seen that Christ does similarly, only that He lays the blame on her first husband, if he divorced her without valid cause.

How can a man cause his wife to commit adultery? The answer is twofold: first by way of public accusation, and second by way of physical need. Concerning the first, if a man divorces his wife it was as if he was publicly declaring she had been unfaithful to him - as was seen in the Law of Moses. And concerning the second, by divorcing his wife, he put her in a very difficult social position; one that essentially required her to find another husband simply to survive. (Isa 3:25-4:1). This is not well appreciated in our day, for we have ovens and laundry machines, and it is relatively easy for a woman to find employment. But in those days, it was near life-threatening for a woman to be left alone. To confirm this, one need only examine all the times the Bible urges kindness to widows in their distress. What then is the state of a woman sent away from her husband? Surely the righteous intent of Joseph intimates how desperate the situation could be, for it says he was unwilling to make Mary a public example, and sought to divorce her secretly.

From this is seen the purpose of the exception clause, namely that in the case of fornication, the man does not cause his wife to become an adulteress; she has already made herself one.

Christ concludes by affirming that remarriage is sin, saying, "whosoever shall marry her that is divorced commits adultery." So then, whether she was put away justly or unjustly, (for both are in the context), anyone that marries a divorced woman commits adultery. Likewise, we must conclude that anyone that marries a divorced man commits adultery, whether he is put away justly or unjustly.

It may be useful to point out that Matthew records two times when Christ spoke about divorce, and both accounts mention the exception clause of fornication. (Mt 5 & 19). But neither Luke nor Mark make any mention of it. (Mk 10, Lk 16). And it is surely with purpose that God inspired Matthew to record this "exception clause," for Matthew is also the only writer that records the account of Joseph seeking to divorce Mary his wife. The reason Joseph was correct in intending to divorce Mary is twofold: first, they were only betrothed; and second, it appeared to Joseph that Mary had been unfaithful, for she was pregnant. Therefore, Joseph was bound by the law to divorce Mary. Now since Matthew identifies Joseph as a righteous man for intending to divorce Mary, it is fitting that Matthew is also the one that identifies that fornication (not adultery) is the only legitimate cause for divorce.

Let us now consider the second passage in Matthew's Gospel. It is a parallel of the account as recorded in Mark 10. The passage begins with Pharisees coming to "tempt" Christ, and asking, "Is it lawful for a man to put away his wife for every cause?" (Mt 19:3). Again, it is obvious from this question that the Jews were taking more liberties in divorce than what the Law allowed. Jesus boldly answered their question by asserting that from the beginning God has joined man and woman together into one flesh: "So they are no more twain, but one flesh. What therefore, God hath joined together, let not man put asunder." (Mt 19:6). Jesus unquestionably asserts both that God hates divorce, and that once a union is consummated, God means it to be for life. The Pharisees, evidently surprised at this strict interpretation, responded with a second question, "Why then did Moses command to give a writing of divorcement, and to put her away?" (Mt 19:7). As has already been mentioned, Jesus responded by pointing out that Moses did not *command* divorce, but *permitted* it because of the hardness of men's hearts.

Jesus continued His answer by again asserting the wickedness of divorce and remarriage, saying, "Whosoever shall put away his wife, except it be for fornication, and shall marry another, committeth adultery, and whoso marrieth her which is put away doth commit adultery." (Mt 19:9). Now it was the disciples' turn to be surprised at this strict interpretation, for they responded by saying, "If the case of the man be so with his wife, it is not good to marry." (19:10).

It is known that these words of Christ, and this comment by the disciples is the source of two interpretations which are contrary to what has been seen thus far. The one interpretation is that a man is allowed to remarry if he divorced his wife because she was unfaithful. The second is that it is good for people to never marry. Are these things true?

Consider the first of these interpretations. Is Christ here granting permission for a man to remarry if he divorces his wife because she was unfaithful? It is not so, as may be seen by closely considering His words. The exception that Christ here mentions is in the context of acceptable causes for divorce, not permission to remarry. (It was the same case in Matthew 5). Nor did Christ say, "If a man put away his wife and marry another, he commits adultery except in the case of fornication." Rather, the exception is after the divorce, not after the conclusion that remarriage is adultery. Further, the exception given is for fornication (unfaithful before marriage), definitely not adultery (unfaithful after marriage). Finally, Christ ended His words by saying, "whoso marrieth her which is put away doth commit adultery." Again, it does not matter why she was put away, for both just and unjust causes are in the preceding sentence. And since it is adultery for a man to marry a divorced woman, it is clearly impossible for her to re-marry without sinning grievously. Of course, all of this is written from the man's perspective, (which is a Scriptural truth - see Gen 5:2 among many others), but applies equally to the woman's perspective (which is also a Scriptural truth - see Gal 3:28). Thus, it is equally wrong for a woman to marry a divorced man, no matter what the cause of the divorce.

And let us consider also the second contrary interpretation. Is Christ here teaching that it is good for people to never marry? A sober study of the text refutes this idea. To properly address this matter, it is best to consider what the disciples said in its broader context. The passage reads:

> Whosoever shall put away his wife, except it be for fornication, and shall marry another, committeth adultery, and whoso marrieth her which is put away doth commit adultery. His disciples say unto him, If the case of the man be so with his wife, it is not good to marry. But he said unto them, All men cannot receive this saving they for whom it is given. For there are some eunuchs which were so born from their mother's womb, and there are some eunuchs which were made eunuchs of men, and there be eunuchs, which

have made themselves eunuchs for the kingdom of heaven. He that is able to receive it, let him receive it.

(Mt 19:10-12)

If we lightly glance on Scripture, we are prone to conclude all sorts of false things. Scripture itself tells us that there are passages that are "hard to be understood," and that if we read as one "unlearned" we will end up twisting them. (2 Pet 3:16). It is no wonder then, that Paul urges Timothy to "Study to shew thyself approved unto God... rightly dividing the word of truth." (2 Tim 2:15).

What is Christ saying? Is He saying that it is better not to marry? Is He telling us that it is super-spiritual to make oneself an eunuch for Christ? These were the errors of those that once promoted monasteries as the ultimate path to heaven. Though the Reformation clearly exposed how serious this error was to the true gospel, sadly it is not uncommon to find this venomous doctrine again rearing its ugly head in protestant churches.

But what then is this text saying? Let us consider it by asking what it was that made the disciples conclude "it is not good to marry"? What had Christ said? He had just said that to divorce and remarry was to commit adultery. Is there anything in this that should make us conclude that a single man should never marry? Not at all. Nothing. Indeed, if the single man marries, and is divorced, and must stay unmarried, then he is only single again, as he first was. So there is certainly nothing to be gained by staying single. Indeed, we observe that the disciples said: "If the case of the man be so with his wife, it is not good to marry." So they are speaking about a man with his wife, not a single man.

It is also to be remembered that the Jews in those days were very evidently taking liberties in divorce that God never intended. It is to be expected, then, that the disciples would also have been surprised at Christ's strict conclusions on divorce and remarriage.

In other words, the disciples concluded: "If the case of the man be so with his wife, it is not good to **re**-marry." The Greek language apparently had no word for *re-marry*. Even in English we use the word *marry* when someone is re-marrying. This is made all the more certain by considering the very chapter now before us, namely 1 Corinthians 7, for Paul repeatedly uses the term *marry* to mean *re-marry*. (ie. "let them marry." 7:9, "if thou marry." 7:28, "let them marry" 7:36, and "she is at liberty to be married." 7:39). Therefore, in agreement with the entire discussion between Christ and the Pharisees, the disciples are brought to see that remarriage after divorce is "not good."

It is useful to again consider the exception clause, "saving for fornication." The KJV translators were certainly correct in translating this as *fornication* - unfaithfulness before marriage, though the Greek might be made somewhat broader in definition. But the Greek word is definitely not *adultery* - unfaithfulness after marriage. As has been seen, Joseph and Mary were considered husband and wife while they were as yet only betrothed. And Joseph justly sought to divorce his wife for her apparent fornication. If one such as Joseph did divorce, would God have allowed him to remarry? Absolutely, for God had not yet joined the two of them into one flesh. But if a marriage is consummated, and one spouse is unfaithful, then divorce is permitted though not recommended. And remarriage is never permitted. It is seen, that all of these exceptions and laws are perfectly consistent with the way Christ worded His answer. Nor do they conflict in the least with either the surprise that the disciples took, nor their conclusion.

But lest some complain about this by referring to Christ's comments about "eunuchs" in the following verses, let us continue considering the matter. Christ affirms the conclusion of the disciples, adding only that it is difficult to accept. And why difficult? It is surely easy to understand how difficult it is for one that is divorced to remain unmarried until his (ex-)wife dies! That this is Christ's meaning is clear, for He goes on to talk about those who make themselves eunuchs for the kingdom of God - that is to say, to avoid the sin of adultery, they remain unmarried indefinitely, thus effectively making themselves a eunuch.

The fact that it is so difficult for a divorced man or woman to remain unmarried, and this even though the charge of adultery looms over their head if they remarry, is all the more proof that Christ was not here advising young people to remain single.

Indeed, Christ points out that not everyone will "receive" (believe) these sayings about divorce and remarriage. Are they then justified? I simply ask: Shall a man be justified by adding unbelief to adultery? By no means! Therefore, let us conclude with the disciples: If it is adultery to marry after a divorce, it is not good to re-marry. And if one find himself in the unpleasant situation of being divorced, let him brace himself to be "a eunuch for the kingdom of God." After all, the apostle Paul in our chapter under study tells widows and widowers that it is "good if they abide" unmarried. If it is good for widows to remain unmarried, how much more is it good for those that have gone through a divorce to stay unmarried.

Finally, let us consider what Christ said to the woman He met by Jacob's well. After a brief conversation, our Lord says to this woman, "Thou hast well said, I have no husband: for thou hast had five husbands; and he whom thou now hast is not thy husband: in that saidst thou truly." (Jn 4:17,18). Here Jesus makes a definite distinction between having a man by marriage and having a man without marriage. The same distinction was made by the prophets in the Old Testament: if a woman committed adultery against her husband, she could repent and return to him again. But if she married another man, she was forbidden from returning to her first husband. The distinction hinges on a marriage, which is, as Malachi puts it, taking a "wife of thy covenant." (Mal 2:14).

In summary, then, Jesus taught that marriage is honourable, divorce is forbidden except in the case of unfaithfulness before marriage, and remarriage is never permitted. Nor should it surprise us that this is exactly what is found in the Law and the Prophets. After all, Christ Himself advised us, saying,

> Think not that I am come to destroy the law or the prophets. I am not come to destroy, but to fulfill. For verily I say unto you, Till heaven and earth pass, one jot or one tittle shall in no wise pass from the law, till all be fulfilled. Whoever therefore shall break one of these least commandments, and shall teach men so, he shall be called the least in the kingdom of God, but whosoever shall do and teach them, the same shall be called great in the kingdom of heaven.
>
> (Mt 5:17-19)

If this is what Christ says of the "least commandment," how much more so the laws regarding marriage and adultery, which are every where held forth as of the greatest importance, and bringing about the greatest punishment for disobedience?

4. What the Apostles Taught

Fourth, and finally, let us consider what the apostles wrote about divorce. It will be remembered that we began this chapter after considering the text: "But and if she depart, let her remain unmarried, or be reconciled to her husband;

and let not the husband put away his wife." (1 Cor 7:11). I trust that the reader will now readily agree that what the apostle here declares is nothing beyond what the Law, the Prophets, and Christ Himself declared, namely that marriage is for life, and remarriage after a divorce is not an option.

But the New Testament, is not any bit behind the Old in making repeated affirmations of these same things. In the epistle to the Romans, the Holy Spirit says,

> For the woman which hath an husband is bound by the law to her husband so long as he liveth, but if the husband be dead, she is loosed from the law of her husband. So then, if, while her husband liveth, she be married to another man, she shall be called an adulteress. But if her husband be dead, she is free from that law, so that she is no adulteress, though she be married to another man.
>
> (Rom 7:2,3).

Words can hardly be more clear. If a woman be married to another man while her husband is still alive, "she shall be called an adulteress." But how can a woman marry another man unless she has divorced her first husband? So then, divorce does not change the definition. Nor does it annul the law of marriage, which lasts until the death of either husband or wife.

And it will be observed that here, as throughout the Scriptures, the grand principles of marriage are used by God to illustrate for us the great spiritual truths of our salvation. Adultery depicts the horrific nature of our revolt from God. Re-marriage after the death of a spouse pictures how Christ's death enables us to be freed from the law so we can be united to Christ. Dear reader, how critical it is, then, that the church understand and apply Scriptural marriage, for Christians, like the priests in Israel, are teachers to all our neighbours by the way we practice marriage.

To the Corinthian church, the apostle writes, "Know ye not that he which is joined to an harlot is one body? For two, saith he, shall be one flesh." (1 Cor 6:16). Here Paul affirms that God's statement concerning the first wedding, namely that God joins the two into one flesh, equally applies if a man goes to a prostitute. The conclusion is staggering. We learn from this that prostitution has lasting consequences. It is also now seen why the Law commanded that if a man seduce a virgin, he must marry her. In other words, whether it be rape, fornication or prostitution, God's declaration is still valid, the two are made one. And what God has joined together, let not man put asunder. Indeed, the very fact that this truth applies even to harlots, is why the apostle Paul is so insistent that Christians must "flee fornication" and have nothing to do with harlots. (1 Cor 6:13-20).

The writer to the Hebrews declares, "Marriage is honourable in all, and the bed undefiled: but whoremongers and adulterers God will judge." (Heb 13:4). When marriage is honoured, divorce is disdained and adultery grievous. And let none pretend that they can commit adultery without the judgment of God finding them out. One need only consider what happened to David because of his adultery with Bathsheba. Though God forgave David his sin, and excused him from the death penalty, yet his family was thereafter plunged so deep into blood and sexual scandals that one is strained to read the accounts. God will not be mocked; He will judge adulterers.

The apostle James also upholds the law of God, saying, "He who said, Do not commit adultery, also said Do not kill.... So speak ye, and so do, as they that shall be judged by the law of liberty." (Jas 2:11,12).

In summary then, the word of God is consistent from beginning to end: the commands of the Law, the teaching of the Prophets, the words of Christ, and the instructions of the apostles are entirely in agreement. Nor should this surprise us, for "all scripture is given by inspiration of God, and is profitable for doctrine...." (2 Tim 3:16). Why should it surprise any that with one Author, (the eternally wise God), and to one profitable purpose, (namely doctrine), all of the Bible agrees with itself? If any be surprised, it is sad proof that something is amiss in the way they handle the Scriptures.

So then, the Scriptures teach that God has designed and ordained marriage. It is to be honoured by all. When the marriage is consummated, God makes the two people one. All who marry are bound to their spouse until death parts them. Man has no right to separate them. God hates divorce. There is only exception to divorce, and that is the case of marital unfaithfulness. If the unfaithfulness occurs before the marriage is consummated, divorce is commanded; if afterwards, divorce is permitted but not recommended. A man may only marry a virgin or a widow. Fornication is a serious sin. Remarriage after divorce is adultery. Adultery is a grievous sin that will face God's judgment and wrath. If a man does get a divorce, he is to remain unmarried until his (ex-) wife dies. God knows how evil and hard-hearted people are, and so He acknowledges that some people will divorce and that others will even marry again. Under no circumstances should a woman return to her first husband after she has married a second man. This is the faithful teaching of Scripture, from cover to cover.

It is appropriate to conclude this chapter with a few practical applications.

First, What should a person do that has committed adultery? He must repent. "Be afflicted and mourn and weep. Let your laughter be turned to mourning...." (Jas 4:9,10). God in Christ Jesus is a forgiving God. Acknowledge your sins. Look to the perfection of Jesus, and believe that He died for sin. Confess your sin to God and cry out to Him for His forgiveness. This is what David did, and God forgave him for his adultery. (See: 2 Sam 11:1-14, Psa 51). God may forgive you too, though you will find yourself bearing painful earthly consequences of your wickedness. (David did. 2 Sam 11:11,14). Repent, therefore, and be faithful to your current spouse. If you are divorced, then commit yourself to remain unmarried until the death of your former spouse. Do not tempt yourself, for "God will judge the adulterer." (Heb 13:4).

Secondly, watch yourself. Solomon repeatedly warned against the seductive, smooth talk of the adulteress woman. Be on your guard, and "remove thy way far from her, and come not nigh the door of her house." (Pr 5:8). Guard your mind too, for Solomon warned, "Lust not after her beauty in your heart..." (Pr 6:25,26). Repent of any evil thoughts you have had in the past. Furthermore, watch yourself lest you fall into the self-righteous error of the Pharisee who prayed: "God, I thank you that I am not like other men ... adulterers...." (Lk 18:11,12). Acknowledge your own sins and your need of Christ's forgiveness.

Thirdly, be willing to welcome other repentant sinners, for Paul wrote: "Know ye not that the unrighteous shall not inherit the kingdom of God? Be not deceived: neither fornicators, nor idolaters, nor adulterers... shall inherit the kingdom of God. And such were some of you, but ye are washed..." (1 Cor 6:9-11).

Fourthly, do not be like the wicked prophets of Jeremiah's day who strengthened evildoers and did not seek to turn people from their wickedness. The Scriptures teach very clearly that we are not "to keep company, if any man that is called a brother be a fornicator, or covetous, or .... with such an one, no not to eat." (1 Cor 5:11). The church must gladly welcome repentant sinners. There is, however, no place in the church for those who claim to be Christians and yet commit adultery without sorrow or repentance. "Put away from among yourselves that wicked person." (1 Cor 5:13). Grieve over this great sin in our day. Grieve over churches that allow adulterers among them without the slightest qualm. Do not strengthen the hand of the guilty, but urge them to repent. Therefore, do not attend a wedding if either the man or his bride has a former spouse that is still alive. Do not condone adultery by attending such a wedding. To condone an adulterous marriage is to strengthen the hands of evildoers.

Fifthly, "marriage is honourable in all." Are you honouring marriage? Honour marriage by encouraging singles to accept that marriage is right for them. Married couples should be encouraged to honour their vows. Discourage people from seeking a divorce. Divorced people should be encouraged to remain unmarried. Be willing to help them financially, if need be, so that they can stay unmarried. Stand against adultery. My friend, God not only forbids adultery, but He commands you to honour marriage. Are you obeying that command? If you are married, are you honouring your own marriage by cherishing only your own spouse? If you have not been honouring marriage, repent and seek the Lord's forgiveness.

CHAPTER 4

More Challenges in Marriage: Unfaithfulness

Having now fully verified that the apostle Paul's prohibition against divorce and remarriage is entirely Scriptural, let us return to this seventh chapter of Paul's first letter to the church in Corinth. The reader will be reminded that we are still in the middle of the second paragraph, (1 Cor 7:8-24), in which Paul particularly deals with some of the challenging issues that married people might face. He began by dealing with the subject of the death of a spouse, and so addressed himself to widows and widowers. Next he dealt with those that experience conflicts within the marriage, and so gave instructions forbidding divorce, permitting only the woman to depart for a time. Finally, we come to a third conflict, namely the topic of an unbelieving spouse. To such, the apostle writes,

> But to the rest speak I, not the Lord: If any brother hath a wife that believeth not, and she be pleased to dwell with him, let him not put her away. And the woman which hath an husband that believeth not, and if he be pleased to dwell with him, let her not leave him. For the unbelieving husband is sanctified by the wife, and the unbelieving wife is sanctified by the husband: else were your children unclean, but now they are holy. But if the unbeliever

depart, let him depart. A brother or sister is not under bondage in such cases: but God hath called us to peace.

(1 Cor 7:12-14)

Here we have an interesting dilemma, for Paul says that it is he that is speaking, not the Lord. Therefore, this is not a command of God, but simply the advice of a fellow believer. But how can we take these words as anything except a command of God? Did we not learn that the prophet Malachi boldly rebuked the Israelites for putting away their pagan wives? And did not Malachi explain his rebuke with the reason: "that He might seek a godly seed"? And is not this the very thing that Paul here uses as an encouragement for believers to dwell with unbelievers? But if the two passages are saying the same thing, why would Paul say, "I speak, not the Lord"?

It is not that there is anything wrong with Paul's advice. The problem is: Why is it advice and not the command of God? If it is only advice, for example, then a man can choose to divorce his unbelieving wife. But can he? I freely admit that I was stumped by this for some time. But after prayer and reflection on this passage, it suddenly dawned on me while I was reading the Greek text that to change the translation of one Greek word to something that is equally valid, the text takes a different meaning, and the dilemma is immediately solved. A brief excursion, therefore, into the interesting world of Greek and English translations may be of benefit.

What is here translated as "he that believeth not," is one Greek word, *apistos*. This word is frequently translated as *unbelievers*. For instance: "and that before *unbelievers*" (1 Cor 6:6). And again, "those that are unlearned, or *unbelievers*" (1 Cor 14:23). And again, "do not be unequally yoked with *unbelievers*" (2 Cor 6:14). Moreover, the word *apistos* is held in opposition to the word *pistos*. (The reader will recall that a leading alpha in Greek is a prefix like the English un-.) Thus, for example, we read, "What part hath he that believeth (*pistos*) with an infidel (*apistos*)?" (2 Cor 6:15). In all these texts, the word *apistos* clearly refers to non-Christians; people lacking in genuine Christian faith.[3]   And this is precisely how the KJV translators took the word here in the text now before us.

---

3   It will be noted from this that the leading alpha in the Greek does not always so perfectly "denote privation," for here *apistos* does not refer to people that had faith and lost it, but to those that have never had Christian faith. Thus, *believer* and *un-believer* is perfectly acceptable as a translation of *pistos* and *apistos*.

Both Moulton and Strong's agree that *pistos* may mean either *believer* or *faithful*. And likewise, both agree that *apistos* may mean either *unbeliever* or *unfaithful*. As *faith* and *belief* mean the same in English, it is easy to admit that the distinction between *believer* and *faithful* is small. However, in English we usually make a great distinction between the word *faithful* and *full of faith*. The word *faithful* means trustworthy, while the phrase, *full of faith* means having a good measure of belief in God. And depending on how closely one examines these two, some might even try to make them sound as tending to opposite extremes. Nevertheless, *faith-ful* and *full-of-faith* may both be used to translate the Greek word *pistos*. Likewise, *unfaithful* and *unbeliever* may both be used to translate the word *apistos*.

If we consider the use of the word *pistos,* it may shed some light on its opposite, *apistos*. As was mentioned above, *pistos* may mean *faithful*. Thus, for example, we read, "God is *faithful"* (1 Cor 1:9). And again, "It is required in stewards, that a man be found *faithful."* (1 Cor 4:2). Again, "I have sent unto you Timothy... who is *faithful* in the Lord." (1 Cor 4:17). Again, in the very chapter of our text, "I give my judgment, as one that hath obtained mercy of the Lord to be *faithful."* (1 Cor 7:25). In each case, the word translated *faithful* is the Greek word, *pistos*. And one would be hard-pressed indeed to have translated it with the English word *believer* in these cases. What, for instance, would be the sense of "God is a believer"? Nor is Paul saying that stewards must be believers, but that they must be trustworthy.

Having therefore established that *pistos* may mean *faithful,* and that *apistos* is the opposite word, it is concluded that *apistos* may mean *unfaithful*. Again, both Moulton and Strong's openly concur with this conclusion. Nevertheless, I could not find a single occurrence in the KJV of where *apistos* was translated as *unfaithful*. The closest I could find is that text which says, "Why should it be thought a thing incredible (*apistos*) with you, that God should raise the dead?" (Acts 26:8). Here the word *incredible,* does not mean amazing, as so many people use the word today, but it means not worthy of credit, untrustworthy. And it is clear that the KJV translators correctly chose not to translate it as *unbeliever* in this instance.

I am not suggesting that the KJV is in error in the way they translated *apistos* in our chapter at hand. Not at all. Indeed, it is clear from the context that the person in question is an unbeliever, for the apostle immediately asks, "How knowest thou, O man, if thou shalt save thy wife?" (vs 15). Further, there is no problem taking the text exactly as the KJV has it, for what is said is entirely true, and supported by the prophet Malachi, as has been shown. The only issue is that then the text is in fact the command of God, not simply the advice of Paul. Indeed, some preachers have taken this passage as a command, though Paul distinctly says otherwise.

Furthermore, it is clear from the book of Acts, that in some cases entire households became believers, but in other cases only the husband or the wife believed. Therefore, it is certain that in the Corinthian church there would have been homes in which only one spouse was a believer. Such homes would surely have issues to deal with, and it is no surprise that Paul would address such.

But since the Greek word may be equally translated with either of two English words, the text should also be considered in light of the second usage. The word *unbeliever* carries with it certain connotations to the average English mind. Likewise, the word *unfaithful* means certain things to English speaking people. Both are correct translations of the Greek; though once translated, the English reader may be deprived of the full sense of the original.

Therefore, with all of this in mind, I invite the reader to re-consider the text before us, this time translating *apistos* with the word *unfaithful* instead of *unbeliever*. In this case, the text reads:

> But to the rest speak I, not the Lord: If any brother hath an unfaithful wife, and she be pleased to dwell with him, let him not put her away. And the woman which hath an unfaithful husband, and if he be pleased to dwell with him, let her not leave him. For the unfaithful husband is sanctified by the wife, and the unfaithful wife is sanctified by the husband: else were your children unclean, but now they are holy. But if the unfaithful depart, let him depart. A brother or sister is not under bondage in such cases: but God hath called us to peace.
>
> (1 Cor 7:12-15)

I trust that the reader will immediately see how this allowable switch of the word *unbeliever* to *unfaithful* makes a significant difference in the English. And after what was said in the preceding chapter on divorce, I hope that the reader can also immediately see why the dilemma is resolved. For, in chapter three above, it was seen that there is only one cause for divorce, namely unfaithfulness in marriage. In the case of unfaithfulness before the wedding, divorce is commanded. But in the case of unfaithfulness after the wedding, divorce is allowed of God, but not recommended. And so we can now see why Paul says it is him speaking and not the Lord. God does not command a man to stay with his wife if she has been unfaithful to him. God only recommends it - as Paul does here. The reader is reminded of the noble example of the prophet Hosea, who received his adulterous wife back to illustrate the love of God toward his straying people.

Not only does it demonstrate true Christlike love to receive back an unfaithful spouse, but Paul particularly tells us that it has ramifications both on the erring spouse, and on the children of the marriage. "The unfaithful husband is sanctified by the wife." What an interesting expression. Indeed, in verse 16 the apostle poses the question,

> For what knowest thou, O wife, whether thou shalt save thy husband? or how knowest thou, O man, whether thou shalt save thy wife?
>
> (1 Cor 7:16)

Why does Paul talk about salvation here? It is because of what he had written several verses earlier: "Be not deceived: neither fornicators, nor ... adulterers.... shall inherit the kingdom of God." (1 Cor 6:9,10). Adultery is no minor incident. It cannot be hid under a rug and forgotten. A man that commits adultery has certainly placed himself in the camp of the unsaved. And as Paul says here, who knows if such an unbeliever will be saved? Salvation is possible, however, for David committed adultery and was saved. And some in Corinth had, and were washed. But there is no guarantee, at least not from our perspective and limited knowledge of the future, as this text makes clear.

But since adulterers do not inherit the kingdom of God, it should be a very rare thing for true believers to fall into this sin. Indeed, the reader will recall that the command, "Thou shalt not commit adultery," is not technically a command, but a statement of future reality. The Christian, therefore, will not commit adultery. Reality tells us that it occasionally does happen, as even the context of this chapter reveals (1 Cor 5). But notwithstanding the rare exception among Christians, adultery is primarily the practice of unbelievers. Therefore, it is certain that the unfaithful spouse mentioned in our text was also an unbeliever. As has been pointed out, the Greek word *apistos* contains both these concepts. I conclude then, that this is what the apostle meant. If this be added to the fact that Corinth was a city notorious for sexual sins, it is concluded that unbelieving spouses were being unfaithful to their Christian husband/wife, causing all sorts of grief in that church. Evidently, the church had written to Paul asking for advice on how to deal with this problem.

How important it really is, then, for the faithful spouse to receive back the unfaithful partner! For it is by such a demonstration of genuine Christian love, that there is hope that the erring partner will be saved, and "sanctified by the faithful wife/husband." The apostle Peter writes similarly of the potential influence of true godliness in marriage, saying, "Likewise, ye wives, be in subjection to your own husbands, that if any obey not the word, they also may without the word be won by the conversation [ie behaviour] of the wives." (1 Pet 3:1).

But the benefit of such a demonstration of Christian love is not limited to the unfaithful partner; it extends also to the children, making them "holy". In this day of abundant divorce, who does not know, who has not heard, of the tragic emotional pain inflicted on children when they see their parents divorce? How much worse if the parents claim to be believers? And how much worse yet if the divorce was caused because one of the parents committed adultery? It is no surprise that in such cases the children would be adversely affected spiritually, and be unholy. But as the influence of a godly mother on her children is universally acknowledged in the Scriptures, so when a faithful partner demonstrates such a depth of Christian love as to receive back an unbelieving, unfaithful spouse, God is willing to declare the children "holy." (See, for example, Prov 31:10-31)

But what if the unfaithful spouse is not willing to live with the faithful partner any more? The apostle writes: "But if the unfaithful depart, let him depart. A brother or sister is not under bondage in such cases: but God hath called us to peace." (7:15) It is not certain whether the unfaithful person will be saved. It is equally uncertain whether an adulterer will be "pleased to dwell with" his wife again. It is possible that the unfaithful party will voluntarily depart. The faithful spouse should simply permit it.

And lest the reader be led to confusion, a reminder is made of the fact that the Scriptures everywhere condemn remarriage after divorce, affirming it to be adultery. Therefore, the remaining spouse, though abandoned, as it were, is called to remain unmarried. This is the sense of Christ when He said, "some have made themselves eunuchs for the kingdom of God." Indeed, the apostle does **not** say, "A brother is loosed from his wife in such cases," but, "A brother in not under bondage in such cases." The word *bondage* means to 'enslave, to reduce to servitude, oppress,' and evidently refers to a state of the mind if the believer tries incessantly to restore the marriage. It is very different from the word *bind,* whereby a man is bound by the law to his wife until death. The distinction is affirmed by the last phrase: "God hath called us to peace," that is, to live peacefully with others in so far as we are able (Rom 12:18), and to have peace in our hearts (Col 3:15).

Why should God allow such a thing? And how can God expect us to have peace in our heart after an unbelieving, unfaithful spouse leaves? And why can a man not know if he will save his unbelieving wife? It is to these questions that the apostle next turns.

CHAPTER 5
The Sovereignty of God

We are still studying the second paragraph of our chapter. And the reader is reminded that the apostle is dealing with the challenging issues that married people might face. Paul first addresses widows and widowers, and so deals with the issue of the death of a spouse. Next the apostle deals with general conflicts in the marriage, and so addresses married people, forbidding them to divorce. Finally, the apostle deals with unfaithfulness in marriage, gently encouraging the faithful partners to graciously allow the unfaithful spouse to dwell with them.

In dealing with these challenges, the issue of the Sovereignty of God has repeatedly surfaced. Why are some able to contain themselves and others not? Why has God given to some one gift, and to others another? Why does God allow one spouse to die first instead of the other? Why does God allow some couples to live into their old age, while others loose a spouse in their youth? Why are some couples happy and others repeatedly at odds with each other? Why do some wives have the displeasure of living with a man so unbearable that she feels obliged to leave him for her own safety? Why do some have to endure an unfaithful partner and others not? Why is it that sometimes whole households believe in the Lord, while at other times only one spouse believes? Indeed, the apostle himself asks similar questions, saying, "What knowest thou, O wife, whether thou shalt save thy husband? And how knowest thou, O man, whether thou shalt save thy wife?"

What are the answers to these questions? There are none. At least, there are none from our perspective. Paul's own questions are evidently meant to mean that neither the husband nor the wife can know if their unbelieving spouse will be saved. But if these fearful questions exist, and if it is impossible to discover an answer, how shall we deal with them? How can God "call us to peace in such cases"? It is surely with this in mind that the apostle enters into a necessary excursion, discoursing on the sovereignty of God, and our response to it. The apostle writes,

> But as God hath distributed to every man, as the Lord hath called every one, so let him walk. And so ordain I in all the churches. Is any man called being circumcised? Let him not become uncircumcised. Is any called in uncircumcision? Let him not be circumcised. Circumcision is nothing, and uncircumcision is nothing, but the keeping of the commandments of God. Let every man abide in the same calling wherein he was called. Art thou called being a servant? Care not for it; but if thou mayest be made free, use it rather. For he that is called in the Lord, being a servant, is the Lord's freeman. Likewise also he that is called being free, is Christ's servant. Ye are bought with a price: be not ye the servants of men. Brethren let every man wherein he was called, therein abide with God.
>
> (1 Cor 7:17-24)

The apostle begins: "But as God hath distributed to every man, as the Lord hath called every one, so let him walk." The answer to all the questions raised by this chapter of Scripture is that God is sovereign. "Whatsoever the Lord pleased, that did he in heaven, and in earth, in the seas, and all deep places." (Psa 135:6). Does a man have gifts? They are called gifts because they are given by God. (Jas 1:17). Shall we complain because of God's generosity or wisdom? (Mt 20:15). "The most High ruleth in the kingdom of men, and giveth it to whomsoever he will, and setteth up over it the basest of men." (Dan 4:17). Therefore, let all people humbly accept that all the variations of life, and certainly as it relates to marriage, are because of God, who distributes things to people as He so pleases. We have no right to argue. We have no ground for objection. Our duty is simply to walk in accordance with whatsoever lot God has given us.

The apostle provides four specific examples of God's calling, namely Jew, Gentile, slave and free. (Paul uses the term circumcision and uncircumcision for Jew and Gentile, as is common in the Scriptures: compare Gal 2:7 with

Acts 15). The four callings here listed are only a few samples of many. Thus, for example, Paul elsewhere adds the obvious, male and female. Writing to the Galatians, Paul says, "There is neither Jew nor Greek, there is neither bond nor free, there is neither male nor female, for ye are all one in Christ." (Gal 3:28). Paul does not there deny the reality of the existence of these six classifications, but points out that all, no matter what their calling, become the children of God in the same way: by faith in Jesus Christ. (Gal 3:25). Indeed, the text acknowledges these six callings, by referring to them in this way, showing that in spite of their reality, there is no distinction in the matters of eternal salvation. Paul says the same things to the church in Colosse (Col 3:11. See also 1 Cor 12:13).

How is it that a man is a Jew? How is it that a man is a Gentile? It is because God determined as much for each person in their birth, as the Scripture says, "God hath made of one blood all nations of men for to dwell on all the face of the earth, and hath determined the times before appointed, and the bounds of their habitation." (Acts 17:26). Words could not be more clear that it is God that determined not only who would be born a Jew and who would be born a Gentile, but also where and when they would be born. What if one is born a Gentile? Shall he try to become a Jew? There is no need, and it is forbidden, as the apostle explains in our text: "Is any called in uncircumcision? Let him not be circumcised."

Having dealt somewhat with the topic of Jew and Gentile, the apostle also makes a few comments about slave and free. Some are born as servants, others are born free. For the Western world, this distinction has mostly faded into the obscure past. This is a good thing, for the Holy Spirit revealed, saying, "but if thou mayest be made free, use it rather." Indeed, freedom is commanded us, if we have the option: "Ye are bought with a price: be not ye the servant's of men." Nevertheless, some do not have that option. That is their lot, their calling. "Care not for it." says our text. Whatever our calling, it should not bother us in the least, for it is of God, and hidden in the great depth of the mysteries of His eternal wisdom. And so the apostle concludes: "Brethren let every man wherein he was called, therein abide with God."

The point is this: It is God's divine privilege to determine these things. And how should we respond? It is just this: "Circumcision is nothing, and uncircumcision is nothing, but the keeping of the commandments of God." Therefore, whatever our lot is, we must walk in it, striving to keep God's commandments. It should be noted, however, that sometimes it might be possible to change our lot. Thus Paul writes to slaves, saying, "but if thou mayest be made free, use it rather." (7:21). And later he says, "Be not ye the servants of men." (7:23). In the first case, a man is a slave by the oppression of other men, in the second, by his own folly. And either way, the "lot" of slavery should be avoided, if possible. We learn from this, therefore, that sometimes we fall into a bad lot, not so much because God wanted us to, but because of our own poor decisions. And we also learn that God expects us, no matter what the cause of our lot, to change it to a better lot if at all possible within the commands of God.

Let us put all these conclusions to work by applying it to the context of our chapter. Does a husband discover his wife has been unfaithful? And does she refuse to live with him any longer? Then that is his lot. Let him keep God's commands, and remain unmarried until the death of his spouse. Does a man suddenly lose his beloved wife, and find himself at a loss in the world? That is his lot. Let him keep God's commands by considering abiding unmarried if he can, or by marrying another if need require. Is a man young and single? That is his lot. But let him marry, for so God has commanded. Does a wife discover she is married to a man that is intolerable to live with? That is her lot. Let her keep God's commands, and submit to her husband as much as possible. But if unable, she must either remain unmarried or be reconciled to her husband. And maybe this lot was of her own folly, for she herself might have chosen him for her husband. In this case, she should acknowledge her folly to the Lord, and still accept her lot.

Moreover, some unfortunate lots might be avoided, or one might escape out of them, as a slave might get free. Does a widower find himself tempted strongly? Then let him avoid that lot, and marry again. Does a wife find her husband unbearable? Maybe it is not so much her lot from God, as it is because she has not been as submissive as God designs. Let her, in such a case, learn from this unpleasant "lot", that she might escape it by influencing her husband with true godliness. (1 Pet 3:1). Many more things could be said, but I pass it by, encouraging the inquisitive reader to make avail of that refreshing and insightful book by Thomas Boston, entitled: *The Crook in the Lot*.

We must now turn our attention to the third and last paragraph of our chapter.

CHAPTER 6

Remarriage

The reader is reminded that in the first paragraph, the apostle addresses singles and those first married. (7:1-7). In the second paragraph, various struggles that married people might face are dealt with. In particular, the apostle deals with the death of a spouse, and so addresses widows and widowers. (7:8,9). He deals with conflicts between spouses, and so addresses married people generally. (7:10,11). And then he deals with unfaithfulness in the marriage, and so speaks to husbands and wives dealing with their unbelieving partner. (7:12-16). The apostle ended his second paragraph by directing our minds to the sovereign power and wisdom of God. We are urged to submit to whatever lot God has assigned us, and to keep His commandments.

We come now to the third and last paragraph of our chapter. (7:25-40). Here the apostle deals with certain issues that might arise in the matter of remarriage. Let us consider the first few verses of this paragraph.

> Now concerning virgins, I have no commandment of the Lord, yet I give my judgment as one that hath obtained mercy of the Lord to be faithful. I suppose therefore that this is good for the present distress, I say, that it is good for a man so to be. Art thou bound unto a wife? Seek not to be loosed. Art thou loosed from a wife? Seek not a wife. But and if thou marry, thou hast not sinned, and

if a virgin marry, she hath not sinned. Nevertheless such shall have trouble in the flesh; but I spare you.

(1 Cor 7:25-28)

It is not immediately obvious who Paul is here particularly addressing. Nor is it particularly obvious what the topic of that address is. Indeed, there have been notable men in the past that have thought this text applied to single men, concluding that if there is almost any distress in the church or world, it is better for them not to marry. It is necessary, therefore, to consider more closely who the apostle is here addressing, lest we apply the text to some group it was not meant for. And it is necessary to consider what the topic of this address is.

Let us begin, therefore, by asking who Paul is addressing in this paragraph. Observe what is written: "It is good for a *man* so to be." And, Paul says, "Art *thou* bound unto a wife? Seek not to be loosed. Art *thou* loosed from a wife? Seek not a wife." (7:26). It is clear from this that Paul is specifically addressing men. And he is speaking to two classes of men, namely those "bound unto a wife," and those "loosed from a wife." By "bound," Paul means married, for at the end of this chapter he writes, "A woman is *bound* by the law as long as her husband liveth." (7:39a). And by "loosed" he means those men whose wife died, for he also writes, "If her husband be dead, she is at *liberty* to be married." (7:39b) Or, as it says elsewhere, "The woman which hath an husband is *bound* by the law to her husband so long as he liveth; but if the husband be dead, she is *loosed* from the law of her husband." (Rom 7:2).

Furthermore, in the last two verses of this paragraph, we find a few short comments about married women and widows. Therefore, in this third paragraph, the apostle is addressing married men and widowers, and married women and widows, with a particular focus on widowers, and to a less extent widows.

But the apostle is *not* addressing single men that have never married. Single men were addressed in the first paragraph, and to them it was commanded, "To avoid fornication, let every man have his own wife." (7:2). Rather, the apostle is addressing men that have been married, whether they still are, or whether they be a widower.

Having established that the apostle is primarily addressing married men and widowers, it remains to be seen what the topic of that address is. Again, observe what is written. The paragraph begins, "Now concerning virgins."

(7:25). Then a few verses later, Paul says, "And if a virgin marry, she hath not sinned." (7:28). And again, near the end of the paragraph, Paul writes, "if any man think that he behave himself uncomely toward his virgin...." (7:36). It is clear from these things that the paragraph deals with one main topic, namely the marriage of a widower to a virgin.

The way Paul has written this paragraph makes it is quite possible for the casual reader to miss both who was being addressed (married men and widowers), and the topic (their marriage to a virgin). However, the reader is reminded that this chapter was written in response to a letter Paul received from the Corinthians - a letter lost to history. The church in Corinth would have known exactly who Paul was addressing, and what the issues were behind his comments. But since we do not have their letter, we must give ourselves to this careful study of the context to discern these issues. The reader is encouraged to re-read the chapter, and particularly this third paragraph (vs 25-40), to assure himself of these things. And if it still remains unclear to the reader, patience is requested, for these things will be confirmed as the text is considered verse by verse.

So then, Paul is addressing married men and widowers. The topic of address is remarriage, and particularly marriage to a virgin. It is cause for reflection that the Holy Spirit inspired Paul to write all these verses about married men and widowers as it concerns marrying virgins. So let us return again to the text, and consider it with new zeal, praying that the Holy Spirit may enlighten our minds to understand these things. The paragraph begins:

> "Now concerning virgins, I have no commandment of the Lord, yet I give my judgment as one that hath obtained mercy of the Lord to be faithful."
>
> (1 Cor 7:25).

Therefore, the instructions that follow are not commands of God, but advice from a fellow believer. And in particular, they are advice from a man that has been approved by God, and found faithful. Therefore, the advice is worthy of our attention and serious consideration. And we learn from this, that even when a believer has several viable options in front of him, it is important to exercise caution about who we give ear to. It is better to give heed to a godly and wise man, than an unstable or ignorant man in the church. (See also: 1 Cor 16:15,16, Titus 1:10,11). Paul continues, saying:

> I suppose therefore that this is good for the present distress, I say,
> that it is good for a man so to be. Art thou bound unto a wife? Seek
> not to be loosed. Art thou loosed from a wife? Seek not a wife.
>
> (1 Cor 7:26)

The advice seems simple enough. The married man is encouraged not to seek
to be loosed from his wife. And the widower is encouraged not to seek a new
wife. But is it really that simple? Why should Paul counsel a married man not
to seek to be loosed from his wife? After all, Paul himself, and only a few verses
earlier, had expressly told us that God forbids a man from divorcing his wife:
"I command, yet not I but the Lord... Let not the husband put away his wife."
(7:10,11). Since this is so, why does Paul say here in verse 26 that this is not
a command of God, but his own judgment? Moreover, what is this "present
distress" that Paul refers to? And why does the apostle use it as the primary
reason for his advice? Moreover, two other times in this chapter Paul advises
widowers not to remarry, but never with the reason of a "present distress" -
why not? These questions force us to again dig deeply into the matter.

In the book of Acts, which spans the entire history of Paul's visits and letters
to Corinth, there is not the least hint of any unusual "distress" in Corinth.
Rather, as Acts makes clear, Paul was in Corinth for the long time of 18
months because the Lord had told him, "no man shall ... hurt thee, for I have
much people in this city." (Acts 18:9). Nor does Paul's letter to the Corinthians
reveal any particular distress worthy of such notice or comment, except what
we find in the immediate context.

Indeed, the last thing that Paul had said about marriage in the preceding
paragraph concerned an unfaithful spouse departing from a believing partner.
And Paul ended with that terrible question, "How knowest thou, O man,
whether thou shalt save thy wife?" (7:16). It is most reasonable, therefore, to
suppose that the "present distress" refers to the matter of unfaithful spouses,
and particularly when an unfaithful spouse no longer desires to live with
his/her wife/husband. Given that Paul is responding to a letter from the
Corinthians, it is self-evident that these were real and important issues in
their church. Further, the city of Corinth was particularly known for being an
immoral city. And the fact that Paul's letter addresses so many basic issues of
church and godliness, it is clear that the church had numerous recent converts
from among the Gentile population. Therefore, it is fully to be expected
that this problem of unfaithful spouses leaving their believing partners had

become an issue among them. None can deny that this would have produced a great and present distress in that church.

Let us return to Paul's advice. Paul gives different advice to each of two classes of men: those bound to a wife, and those loosed. To the married man, he writes, "Are thou bound unto a wife? Seek not to be loosed." If the "present distress" is indeed that unfaithful spouses were leaving their believing partners, then this advice is perfectly to be expected. It has already been pointed out that the law forbids a man from divorcing his wife except for one reason: namely unfaithfulness on the part of his wife. We have seen from multiple places of Scripture, that God does not forbid such a man from divorcing his wife. Yet we have also seen that God recommends he not do so. It is precisely the same here. Paul expressly tells us that this is not a command of God, but good advice. A man may "seek to be loosed from" his unfaithful wife. But Paul counsels against it.

However much the man "bound to a wife" is permitted to divorce her if she has been unfaithful to him, he is not permitted to remarry. Paul advises such a man not to seek to be loosed. But if this advice is ignored, no more permission is granted to the man. Indeed, as has been seen, only death frees a man or woman from the law of marriage: "A woman is bound by the law to her husband as long as he liveth." (Rom 7:2). And if anyone that divorces his wife marries after such a divorce, he commits adultery: "Whosoever putteth away his wife and marries another, committeth adultery." (Lk 16:18).

It is seen, then, that Paul's advice is nothing new to the Scriptures, though it was surely new to the believing Gentiles in Corinth. Indeed, it is to be frankly assumed that every believer in Corinth that had an unbelieving, unfaithful spouse was a recent convert, and a Gentile. (Believing Jews were not known for adultery. And God forbids His people from marrying anyone outside the faith.)

Paul next turns his attention to that of the widower, saying, "Art thou loosed from a wife? Seek not a wife." (7:27). Here again, as with several other places in this chapter (vs 8 & 40), Paul's advice is that widowers remain single. And again, Paul has consistently made it clear that this is not a command of God, but only advice from a fellow believer.

It may be observed that Paul is addressing two different men: the one bound to his wife, and the one loosed from his wife. The two are not the same. The first, the one bound to a wife, was advised by Paul not to seek to be loosed. If he resisted the advice and sought to be loosed, then it was of his own volition and action. But the second man, the one loosed from his wife, is someone that was loosed by the act of something else. (The Greek is in the Passive voice). Now the only thing that can loose a man without his acting a part is the death of his wife, for that alone frees a man from the law of marriage. The English somewhat obscures this significant distinction, but the reader will note that there is a huge difference between, "Art thou loosed from a wife?" as Paul expressed it, and "Did thou loose thyself from thy wife?" or, "Did thou put away thy wife?" as would have been the case if the apostle was speaking about a man that chose to divorce his wife.

So then, Paul here addresses two types of men: married men and widowers. Concerning the married man, it is understood from the context that his wife had committed adultery against him. Paul advises such a man not to seek a divorce. And the advise given to the widower is that he not seek a wife. When the apostle gave the same advice earlier (vs 8), he left us with no explanation. But here, under the inspiration of the Holy Spirit, Paul expends himself in the next 8 verses to provide systematic reasons for his counsel. But first, he assures the widower, saying,

> But and if thou marry, thou hast not sinned, and if a virgin marry, she hath not sinned. Nevertheless such shall have trouble in the flesh; but I spare you.
>
> (1 Cor 7:28).

Once again Paul confirms that God does not forbid a widower from remarrying, for we are expressly told that it is not sin if he does. And consistent with the topic of this paragraph, we observe that Paul deals only with the issue of marrying a virgin. Thus, Paul testifies to the fact that it is not sin for a widower to marry a virgin.

It was pointed out above, and it will be referred to again later on, that since Paul is speaking in broad generalities in this chapter, it is taken for granted that a widow or widower is of somewhat advanced age. Likewise, it was pointed out that God commands all to marry, and particularly to marry young. Therefore, it is taken for granted that the virgin here spoken of is a young woman. The conclusion is that it is not sin for an older man to marry a young virgin. However much this is looked down on in our modern day, this practice has been common in history, and is frequently found in the Bible, even among the godly. The questioning reader may prove this to himself by simply reading about the Patriarchs in the book of Genesis, and of the godly in Israel. By using the ages and dates mentioned, the reader is able to determine the age spread between husband and wife. And it is affirmed here in our chapter that such a practice is not sin.

Paul here mentions that if a widower marries a virgin, they will have trouble in the flesh. Here is Paul's first reason behind why a widower is advised not to remarry. No detail is provided regarding what type of "trouble" such a couple might expect, only that it is not a spiritual trouble, but "trouble in the flesh." It is reasonable to suppose that at least part of this fleshy trouble is that if an older widower marries a young virgin, they must expect children. And children, though a great joy, and though given to older men like Abraham, can no doubt be somewhat of a physical challenge to an older man. Other physical troubles might be mentioned, but as Paul says nothing, the reader is invited to ponder this on his own.

Having thus affirmed that it is not sin for a widower to marry a virgin, the apostle turns to instruct his readers with spiritual truths relating to marriage, still keeping the topic of remarriage and virgins in particular view. The apostle writes,

> But this I say, brethren, the time is short: it remaineth that both they that have wives be as though they had none; and they that weep, as though they wept not; and they that rejoice, as though they rejoiced not; and they that buy as though they possessed not; and they that use this world as not abusing it: for the fashion of this world passeth away.
>
> (1 Cor 7:29-31)

Here, in beautiful and heavenly language, the apostle lifts our minds from our lowly problems and questions, by reminding us that all these things of the earth are but short and temporary. Whatever our lot on the earth, believers live with such a view of God and Christ that it might appear that our lot is quite different. Was Paul poor? Yet did he make many rich. Does the world view Paul as a deceiver? Yet does he speak the truth. Does a believer sorrow? Yet does he rejoice in Christ. (2 Cor 6:9,10). And so must the Christian view marriage. Is he first married? It appears as if he has no wife. Does his wife die? It appears as if he does not mourn. Does he remarry? It appears as if he does not rejoice.

Is Paul advising us to live in a state of denial? Of course not. The Scriptures everywhere testify to these realities: marriage in one's youth, sorrow when one's wife dies, joy in remarriage, and so forth. Even this text here says, "they rejoice," and "they mourn." But it is "as though" they do not. The believer lives with much greater things as his primary focus: "If ye then be risen with Christ, seek those things which are above, where Christ sitteth on the right hand of God." (Col 3:1). Christ spoke similarly when he said, "If anyone come to me and hate not his father, and mother, and wife, and children, and brethren, and sister, yea, and his own life also, he cannot be my disciple." (Lk 14:26). What? Shall a man hate his wife? Of course not, for God commands a man to love his wife. But the Christian's love for God and thoughts of heaven make him so new, so different, that it is as if he had no wife, as if he hated her. "Therefore if a man be in Christ, he is a new creature, old things are passed away; behold, all things are become new." (2 Cor 5:17). So new, that even the buying and possessing of mundane things is transformed, and it appears we own nothing!

Let the reader reflect on these things. And let each of us ask if such things be true in our own heart. Are our minds set on earthly things, and only from time to time do we drag our attention from off these our pleasures to look up into heaven? Have we planned for a long and happy life, engaging in this business and that, not recognizing how short our life really is? Do we cling to our possessions, forgetting that soon we shall go to the grave and all that we once possessed will become the property of someone else? How fitting indeed, that the apostle should write these delightful words in the middle of a chapter on human marriage. He could not even write one small chapter without reminding us of how temporary all these things of the earth really are.

It has been pointed out that this paragraph is particularly addressing widowers, and as is usual in the normal course of life, widowers are somewhat advanced in age. How much more fitting, then, is Paul's statement here, "Brethren, the time is short." (7:29) Older men need a gentle reminder that their life is almost done. It is all too easy for such to be overburdened with the death of a lifelong wife, or to be carried away in the joys of a young wife, or to busy themselves in the accumulation of worldly possessions, and to forget that time is short. How sad is the folly of that man who is so concerned with the things of this life that he neglects to see the evidence that he is soon to die. For so writes the prophet Hosea: "Strangers have devoured his strength, and he knoweth it not; yea gray hairs are here and there upon him, yet he knoweth not." (Hos 7:9).

Having reminded us of the brevity and temporality of life, even married life, Paul continues to explain his advice to widowers, saying:

> But I would have you without carefulness. He that is unmarried careth for the things that belong to the Lord, how he may please the Lord. But he that is married careth for the things that are of the world, how he may please his wife. There is difference also between a wife and a virgin. The unmarried woman careth for the things of the Lord, that she may be holy both in body and in spirit; but she that is married careth for the things of the world, how she may please her husband. And this I speak for your own profit, not that I may cast a snare upon you, but for that which is comely, and that ye may attend upon the Lord without distraction.
>
> (1 Cor 7:32-37).

Paul is here contrasting the state of a married man with that of an unmarried man so that the widower may make an informed decision about whether or not to remarry. Likewise, the apostle contrasts the married woman with the unmarried woman. Again, the Greek word for unmarried, *agamos,* is best understood to mean no longer married. This has been clear throughout this chapter, and it is again so here. In this third paragraph, Paul is addressing those bound to and those loosed from a wife: married men and widowers. (7:27). Likewise, Paul ends by addressing married women and widows (7:39,40) Even in this section of the paragraph, before contrasting the married woman from the unmarried woman, Paul expressly states, "there is also a difference between a wife and a virgin." It will be recalled that the Greek word for *wife* also means *woman.* In other words, Paul is contrasting the woman that is a wife, (married) with the woman that was a wife, (unmarried). But he is excluding virgins from this contrast. If it were meant otherwise, Paul would have contrasted the virgin with the married woman, instead of the unmarried with the married. But consistent with the entire chapter, Paul lets his readers know he distinguishes here between a woman and a virgin. And he contrasts a married woman with an unmarried (ie a widow).

Therefore, the apostle is not here contrasting the married state from the unmarried state so that the young, never-married single can conclude he should stay single. Not at all. Rather, the apostle is contrasting these two states to help the widower understand his options, and to help him see the advantage of remaining unmarried.

The apostle provides encouragement, both to widows and to widowers, saying that it is better if they remain unmarried. And when he says, "not that I may cast a snare on you," he once again makes it clear that such is not commanded of them, but only in accordance with good advice.

The contrast made between the married man and the unmarried man is identical to the contrast made between the married woman and the unmarried woman. Married persons, that is, re-married persons, care for the things of the world, how they may please their spouse. But the widow or widower that remains unmarried cares for the things of the Lord.

It is again remarked that this chapter is dealing with broad generalities of life and marriage, so it is taken for granted that the widowers and widows here spoken to are somewhat of an advanced age. With this in mind, it is more readily seen how an unmarried man or woman cares for the things of the Lord. Having married in their youth, and now being of an advanced age, they are at a place in life very different from young singles. They likely have children. They have probably established a home, to some degree. And they are able to serve the Lord with the wisdom that comes with age. All of this is consistent with the Scripture, but it is especially brought out in Paul's letter to Timothy, where younger widows are urged to remarry. Thus, for example, we read that elders are to be men that have raised godly children, have their family in order, are neither young nor new to the faith, and so forth. (1 Tim 3) And when dealing with widows, Paul informs Timothy that only those 60 or over may be listed as widows, that these must be "well reported of for good works, if she have brought up children, if she have lodged strangers...." (1 Tim 5:10) And to such widows, Paul writes, "Now she that is a widow indeed, and desolate, trusteth in God, and continueth in supplications and prayers night and day." (1 Tim 5:5). This is exactly what Paul is commending here in his letter to the Corinthians, namely that widows and widowers are able to concern themselves with pleasing the Lord, "holy in both body and in spirit."

Anyone that has had the privilege of knowing a godly, older widow or widower will readily affirm the unique advantage that such a person has for serving the Lord. They may not have the strength of body to do "chores" like they used to, but they have wisdom and insight, love and gentleness, patience and observation skills. And they can make a profound impact on the people they come in contact with, especially on their children and grand-children.

But we should not assume that such godly behaviour is easy or natural, not even to a widow. Indeed, the apostle warns that some widows "live in pleasure," saying such a woman is "dead while she liveth." (1 Tim 5:6). And this is all the more reason why young people should marry, and why young widows and widowers should marry again. It is in marriage that they may "diligently follow every good work," whether that be raising children, managing household affairs, learning to love one's spouse, or using one's home to care for those in need. (1 Tim 5:10). If the reader cannot see this, he is invited to read 1 Timothy chapters 3 and 5 and Titus chapter 2 with these things in mind.

Paul continues, by saying, "And this I speak for your own profit, not that I may cast a snare upon you, but for that which is comely, and that ye may attend upon the Lord without distraction." (7:35). God has made people differently, and not all can take Paul's advice without finding themselves ensnared. Such people should marry again, as was said earlier: "It is good for them if they abide even as I. But if they cannot contain, let them marry, for it is better to marry than to burn." (7:8,9) But for those widows and widowers that can "contain," it is for their good and profit that they remain unmarried, so that they may serve the Lord in undivided attention.

Paul continues on in this contrast between the married and unmarried, between the one that chooses to re-marry, and the one that chooses to remain unmarried, saying,

> But if any man think that he behaveth himself uncomely toward his virgin, if she pass the flower of her age, and need so require, let him do what he will, he sinneth not: let them marry. Nevertheless, he that standeth steadfast in his heart, having no necessity, but hath power over his own will, and hath so decreed in his heart that he will keep his virgin, doeth well. So then he that giveth her in marriage doeth well; but he that giveth her not doeth even better.
>
> (1 Cor 7:37,38)

The reader, possibly familiar only with modern Western practices of marriage, may not understand that in Paul's day it was a world-wide practice for father's to arrange for the marriage of their sons and virgin daughters. Paul mentions this practice in the last of these verses, saying, "So then he that giveth her [the virgin] in marriage doeth well: but he that giveth her not doeth better." (7:38). Since this is Paul's conclusion of the matter as it relates to men, and since the entire discussion began with the words, "concerning virgins," it is clear that what was happening in Corinth is that father's were betrothing their virgin daughters to older widowers.

Once again the apostle contrasts two men: one that chooses to remarry, and one that chooses not to. In this part of Paul's discourse, both are said to have a "virgin," by which we are to understand that a betrothal has taken place. The apostle concludes that the man that marries "sinneth not" (7:36) but the man that does not marry, "doeth well." (7:37). As the entire contrast, since verse 28, has been with the widower in mind, it is certain that Paul intends the same here. The two men contrasted represent the two options for a widower: to remain unmarried, or to marry his virgin.

The apostle mentions two particular reasons why a widower might choose to marry. First, he says, "if any man think that he behaveth himself uncomely toward his virgin, if she pass the flower of her age..." For those unfamiliar with the practice of arranged marriages, it should be pointed out that frequently marriages were arranged before one of them was old enough to marry. And the widower is particularly instructed that he should wait until the woman is old enough to marry. Here again, it is seen that Paul is dealing with a young virgin and an older man.

Why might the man think he is behaving improperly towards "his virgin," his espoused wife? One need only to think of the virgin to answer this question. The girl is espoused, but not married. It is not known how long the older widower will live. Maybe he will outlive her time of child bearing. Must she then die childless? So then, the first reason for the man to marry is out of kindness and respect for the longings of his espoused wife, "his virgin," to be a mother and wife.

The second reason for the marriage is, "and need so require." This has been Paul's faithful advice, that if a widow or widower "cannot contain, let them marry." The man considering the marriage should consider this not only in his own case, but also in the case of the virgin, for she too might strongly desire and need to marry. And Paul again repeats the conclusion: "he sinneth not: let them marry."

We learn from this that God does not consider it sin when anyone has a need to marry. Nor should any one dare to insult someone, whom God does not condemn. We also learn that neither old age nor widowhood necessarily terminates such a need. And it is again verified that it is not sin for an older widower to remarry, even if he marries a young woman. Therefore, let none judge an older man for marrying a young woman, for God Himself says it is not sin.

After having said these things to the man that chooses to marry, the apostle turns to address the man that chooses not to. Four conditions are made about such a man. First, "he standeth steadfast in is heart." Second, he has "no necessity." Third, he "hath power over his own will." And fourth, the man has "so decreed in is heart that he will keep his virgin." It should be clarified that these instructions are directed to an older widower that has had a virgin betrothed to him. If no such betrothal has taken place, Paul's advice was more simple: "Art thou loosed from a wife? Seek not a wife." And surely part of the reason for such stringent conditions is that a virgin was involved.

This situation of an older man "keeping his virgin" is adequately illustrated in the case of king David and Abishag, his legal concubine. The old king kept Abishag a virgin. Yet she was considered his wife so much so that when David's son asked to marry her, Solomon put him to death for such a wicked request. (Compare 1 Cor 5:1 with 1 Kings 1:1-4, 2:16-23).

Paul concludes, saying that such a widower that keeps his espoused wife a virgin "doeth well." Why does he do well to keep his virgin? As the apostle has now all but finished his discourse as it relates to widowers and virgins, we must make all our conclusions from his preceding comments. We have seen that if such marry, they "will have trouble in the flesh." We have seen that for these older widowers "the time is short." We have learned that "the fashion of this world passeth away." And we have heard that "the unmarried man careth for the things that belong to the Lord; how he may please the Lord." Therefore, such a man does well in that he may devote the last days of his life on earth to pleasing God, to focusing his life on spiritual things, and to spare himself from entangling earthly concerns. Indeed, the prayer of the aged, whether a widower or one still married to the wife of his youth, should be that of the Psalmist: "Now also when I am old and grayheaded, O God, forsake me not; until I have shewed thy strength unto this generation, and thy power to every one that is to come." (Psa 71:18). How beautifully do these words align with the apostle's here in this letter to the Corinthians! Let older men concern themselves, not with worldly pursuits, nor with pleasures, but with passing on the knowledge of God's greatness to the next generation. Of such godly elders the church of every generation stands in need, and is benefitted greatly by them.

If it is not a "sin" for the man to marry his virgin, and if it is also "well" for the other man to keep his virgin, then it is surely not sin for a father to have given his virgin daughter to such a man. And this is exactly what the apostle says next: "So then, he that giveth her in marriage doeth well." We learn from this that it is perfectly good and acceptable for a father to betroth his virgin daughter to an older widower.

But the apostle does not end here. Rather, he finishes by saying, "but he that giveth her not in marriage doeth better." Is the apostle here overthrowing marriage? Is he overthrowing the ancient practice of arranged marriages? Absolutely not. The apostle is not speaking about just any betrothal, but a betrothal to an older widower, as is clear from the context. And why is it better not to betroth in such a case? Surely it is this: the man that he betroths his virgin daughter to might keep her a virgin. And in that case, she has the unfortunate displeasure of living as an espoused woman indefinitely, waiting for her husband to die. And she might pass the age of child-bearing before this happens, in which case she will remain childless. Further, as Paul pointed out, (vs 36) these considerations might make an older widower decide to marry this his virgin, preventing him from spending his last years of life in undistracted service to the Lord.

I trust that the reader will concur that Paul's conclusions here prove beyond any doubt that the discussion in this paragraph has indeed been about older widowers marrying young virgins. Indeed, the last two verses of the chapter verify the matter even further, for the apostle switches from dealing with widowers, to dealing with widows. He does so by saying:

> The wife is bound by the law as long as her husband liveth: but if her husband be dead, she is at liberty to be married to whom she will: only in the Lord. But she is happier if she so abide, after my judgment, and I think also that I have the Spirit of God.
>
> (1 Cor 7:39,40)

Once again, Paul upholds the law of God, affirming that the only thing that releases a wife from the law of marriage is her husband's death. And once again, for it has now been mentioned several times, the apostle informs us that the widow is free to marry, but that "she is happier if she" abide unmarried. Once again I ask the question: Is Paul contradicting himself when he tells Timothy "I will therefore that the young widows marry, bear children...."? (1 Tim 5:14) Paul is not double-tongued, for he has "the Spirit of God," as it says here. The distinction, as was pointed out above, is that in his letter to Timothy, Paul splits widows into two camps: younger widows, and widows 60 and over. Younger widows should remarry. The older widows may remarry if they so choose, but it is not recommended.

It will also be observed from these last words of our chapter that though the widow is at "liberty to be married to whom she will," there is one restriction, namely that she marry a believer. Such has been God's instructions all throughout Scripture. In the Old Testament, for example, the Israelites were forbidden from marrying a foreigner, unless he or she had converted. And elsewhere in the New Testament, it says: "Be ye not unequally yoked together with unbelievers: for what fellowship hath righteousness with unrighteousness? And what communion hath light with darkness? And what concord hath Christ with Belial? And what part hath he that believeth with an infidel?" (2 Cor 6:14,15).

This third and last paragraph of the chapter before us has touched on the topic of arranged marriages. We read of a man choosing whether or not he will marry his virgin. We read of a father giving his virgin daughter in marriage. Yet we read of a widow at liberty to marry "whom she will." What can be made of these things? There is so much to be learned, not only from this chapter, but from many other Scriptures, about arranged marriages and finding a spouse, that it warrants an entire chapter. And it is to this that we now turn.

CHAPTER 7

Arranged Marriages

In the previous chapter we followed through Paul's discourse on remarriage, noting that he was particularly addressing the issue of a widower marrying a virgin. In advising and instructing on this, the matter of arranged marriages was incidentally brought up. With this interesting topic in mind, let us consider again what the apostle writes:

> But if any man think that he behaveth himself uncomely toward his virgin, if she pass the flower of her age, and need so require, let him do what he will, he sinneth not: let them marry. Nevertheless, he that standeth steadfast in his heart, having no necessity, but hath power over his own will, and hath so decreed in his heart that he will keep his virgin, doeth well. So then he that giveth her in marriage doeth well; but he that giveth her not doeth even better. The wife is bound by the law as long as her husband liveth: but if her husband be dead, she is at liberty to be married to whom she will: only in the Lord. But she is happier if she so abide, after my judgment, and I think also that I have the Spirit of God.
>
> (1 Cor 7:36-40)

We learn from this that a widower has the God-ordained right to choose if and when he will marry the virgin that has been betrothed to him, as long as she is old enough to marry. We also learn that a father has the God-ordained right to choose who he will betroth his virgin daughter to. Further, we learn that a widow has the privilege of marrying any one that she wishes to, as long as he is a believer.

Do these lessons startle the reader? I suspect they startle, with rare exception, nearly every professing Christian in North America. Must these conclusions, then, be false, since they are at odds with so great a number of people? It is not so. The conclusions are those of the Scriptures, as stated by the apostle Paul. Maybe, then, Paul's words are at odds with the rest of Scripture? Or maybe he spoke this way to accommodate the local culture in Corinth? Maybe Paul invented these things? Such are the questions our generation might ask.

Owing to the extreme disparity between the way Paul here speaks of marriage and the practices of modern churches in the West, it is worthwhile - no it is fundamentally essential - to consider what the Scriptures teach on this important subject. What do the Scriptures teach? To answer this question, six things will be investigated: *first* how and why marriage was established; *second*, the historical accounts of marriage in the Bible; *third*, the various instructions and comments in the Bible that relate to marriage; *fourth*, the issues of dowries; *fifth*, the various accounts of abuses of this practice; and *sixth*, the likeness between marriage and Christ and His church.

1. How and Why God Established Marriage

Let us begin with the first wedding, and examine how and why God established marriage. Shortly after creating the world, God said, "It is not good that the man should be alone: I will make him an help meet for him." (Gen 1:18). And this God did by creating Eve. After God made Eve, as the Scriptures record, "He brought her unto the man." (Gen 2:22). Then the Lord established marriage with an enduring declaration: "Therefore, shall a man leave his father and his mother and shall cleave unto his wife, and they shall be one flesh." (Gen 2:24). The declaration is enduring in that God would not have any man separate from his wife. But, it is also enduring because it is true for people of every generation. Jesus Christ made both of these points clear when He said:

> But from the beginning of the creation God made them male and female. For this cause shall a man leave his father and mother and cleave to his wife, and they twain shall be one flesh. So then they

are no more twain, but one flesh. What therefore God has joined together, let not man put asunder.

(Mk 10:6-9)

It is observed, therefore, that the account of the first wedding was written down, not to entertain readers, but to establish God's divine pattern for marriage. As Christ pointed out, God joins a man and woman together into one flesh with the intent that no man should ever separate them.

Therefore, based on the words of Christ, the first marriage and God's declarations about it were meant to establish God's eternal will regarding marriage. From this we learn that marriage was instituted because God had graciously noted that "it was not good that the man should be alone." (Gen 2:18) And God, as a Father, established the pattern of arranged marriages by finding a wife for his son, Adam. And God, as the authority of Eve, gave this woman to Adam to be his wife. We also learn from this divine pattern that men should not live alone, nor should they leave their parents without marrying, that marriage is God's gracious intention for the blessing of man, that marriage is for life, and that it is the parents' responsibility to find spouses for their children. It is also seen that the father, (if he is alive, of course), chooses the time of his son's wedding.

It may be further observed that we are not left in the dark concerning God's motives behind the choice of a partner: God noted that it was not good for Adam to be alone; and He noted that Eve was a helper "meet" for Adam. Therefore, parents should not choose spouses for their children to satisfy their own interests (ie wealth, beauty, etc), but with a view to the spiritual and physical blessing of their children.

2. Historical Accounts of Marriage in the Bible

God did not fail in His purposes, nor in this His divine precedent in arranging the first marriage. Indeed, although mankind's failures in the matter of marriage have been so great and so repeated as to fill the earth with sin, yet it is unquestionable that marriage has been universally practised on planet earth by people of all walks of life and religious backgrounds. And along with this interesting and remarkable fact of history is the equally amazing fact that people have almost universally followed the practice of arranging for the marriages of their children by finding wives for their sons and giving their daughters in marriage - just as God did for Adam and Eve.

It is useful to consider this last statement by examining the historical records found in the Bible concerning marriage, and in particular, arranged marriages. Even before the flood, the ungodly men and women who were swept away to their death by those waters arranged for the marriages of their children, at least in some cases. The Lord Jesus Christ testified to this when He said, "For as in the days before the flood, they were eating and drinking, marrying and **giving** in marriage, until the day that Noah entered into the ark." (Mt 24:38 Emphasis added.).   Nevertheless, arranged marriages were not universally practised in the pre-flood days, especially in the last years leading up to the flood. But we will come back to that later.

The historical books of the Bible reveal that arranged marriages were generally common in the Middle East from the time of the flood to the time of Christ. It is evident that certain norms were established, but, as one might expect, they were not always followed. For example, Shechem fell in love with Jacob's daughter Dinah, and raped her. Yet he then had recourse to the proper procedures, and "spake unto his father, saying, Get me this damsel to wife." (Gen 34:4). Nor can anyone dispute that arranged marriages were the norm in Shechem's society, for it was on that basis that he himself urged his town to establish peaceful relations with Jacob's extended family, saying: "Let us take their daughters to us for wives, and let us give them our daughters." (Gen 34:21).

Arranged marriages were also the norm in Egypt. Thus, as soon as Pharaoh had raised Joseph out of prison, he immediately "gave him to wife Asenath the daughter of Potiphera." (Gen 41:5). And, hundreds of years later, another Egyptian Pharaoh did the same thing, this time giving a wife to one Hadad. (1 King 11:19).   Likewise, Hagar, Abraham's Egyptian wife, went back to Egypt to find a wife for her son Ishmael. (Gen 21:21).

The Philistines practised arranged marriages, as is clear from the account of Samson and his first wife. (See Jud 14:2-15:2).

And it is most certain that the Israelites also practised arranged marriages. Abraham, for instance, sent his servant to find a wife for Isaac. Likewise, Rebekah was given to Isaac by her father. (Gen 24). Isaac commanded his son Jacob to take a wife from among Laban's daughters. And likewise, both Rachel and Leah were given to Jacob by Laban. (Gen 28:2, 29:19-27). Judah found a wife for his son Er. (Gen 38:6). Zipporah was given in marriage to Moses. (Ex 2:21). Caleb gave his daughter in marriage to Othniel. (Jos 15:16). Samson's parents got him a wife. (Jud 14:2). Naomi, as a widow, found a husband for her widowed daughter-in-law. (Ruth 3:1-5, 4:3,5). King Saul gave his daughters away in marriage. (1 Sam 18:19, 21). Sheshan gave his daughter to Jarha. (1 Chr 2:35). And Jehoida the priest gave two wives to the young and fatherless king Joash. (2 Chr 24:3).

Nor can we assume these were isolated cases, for the Scriptures expressly tell us it was a general practice in Israel. For instance, in the time of the Judges, we read, "And the children of Israel took... their daughters to be their wives, and gave their daughters to their sons..." (Jud 3:5,6). And reference might also be made to that unique and pathetic story of how the Israelites found wives for the 600 surviving Benjamites after the tribe was nearly destroyed. (Judg 21:1-23). But one of the most interesting proofs of the practice of arranged marriages is the frequency with which a wicked king of Judah is found to be married to a godly woman, who raises up a godly son to succeed his wicked father. Time would fail me to demonstrate this, so I leave it to the reader to observe the pattern in the record of the kings, how a godly king always has a godly mother, though not always a godly father. And how else would an ungodly king marry a godly woman, except the wedding had been arranged for him by his father?

It is certain from all these accounts, that parent-arranged marriages was the established norm, not only in Israel, but in the entire world from the time of Adam until the time that the Bible was completed. Yet, it is also seen from these examples, that sometimes the marriage, though arranged by the parents, was first proposed because of an awareness of someone having fallen in love. Thus, for example, Jacob had fallen in love with Rachel. Shechem had fallen in love with Dinah. Samson had fallen in love with a woman in Timnath. Saul's daughter, Michal, had fallen in love with David.

Since by Adam's fall, "sin has entered the world" (Rom 5:12), it is most certain that men have perverted marriage, whether by rape, or fornication, or adultery. The Scriptures have so many accounts of such sins, it is painful to recount them. But since we have in mind the matter of arranged marriages, it is useful to consider the accounts of those that found a spouse without attending to the normal route of an arranged marriage. Indeed, it is certain that at all times in world history there have been some sons and daughters that rebelled against this practice, and some parents that were slack in taking up their responsibilities. It is particularly of interest to note the outcome of such marriages.

We begin with the pre-flood world. It is remembered that Christ has told us that arranged marriages were practised up until the flood, even by the ungodly. However, the practice was evidently falling into disuse, for the Scriptures record: "The sons of God saw the daughters of men that they were fair, and they took them wives of all which they chose." (Gen 6:2). As there is some confusion about who is being spoken of here, it is useful to consider it. Some claim that the "sons of God" mentioned here refers to angels, because angels are called "sons of God" in the book of Job (Job 1:6). It is true that angels are called "sons of God." However, by looking at the context of this verse in Genesis, it is certain that by "sons of God," Moses meant men. I invite the reader to verify this for himself. Moreover, Adam was called a "son of God." (Lk 3:38). And the Bible expressly calls believers by the same name: "For as many as are led by the Spirit of God, they are the sons of God." (Rom 8:14). Further, pagan women are called in Scripture, "the daughter of a strange god." (Mal 2:11). Moreover, the apostle Paul expressly informs us that "God hath made of one blood all nations of men for to dwell on all the face of the earth...." (Acts 17:26). Also, the word of God expressly tells us, "For as the woman is of the man, so is the man also by the woman; but all things are of God." (1 Cor 11:11,12). Now since that "one blood" is the blood of Adam, and since women only come of man, and men only of woman, it is impossible that angels should have created life by marrying women. Indeed, that is the great splendour and stunning marvel of Christ Jesus: He was born of a virgin by the power of the Holy Spirit. Therefore let us banish the idea that angels married women and had children by them, for it is contrary to the Scriptures.

So then, what this text in Genesis is saying is that men saw that women were beautiful, and married any one they chose. Some writers (notably John Bunyan[4]) have felt that the term "sons of God" particularly referred to men that were followers of the one true God. (Mal 2:11 supports this conclusion.) In this case, the sons of godly parents were marrying whomsoever they chose. I do not object to this position, and it only serves to intensify the reality, namely that the practice of arranged-marriages had fallen into disrepute in those pre-flood days, and even among the children of the godly. In its place men were marrying based on how beautiful a woman looked, and in accordance with what they themselves chose.

What was the result? The very next verse reads: "And the Lord said, My spirit will not always strive with man, for that he also is flesh: yet his days shall be an hundred and twenty years.... And God saw that the wickedness of man

---

4   See Bunyan's Commentary on Genesis.

was great in the earth." (Gen 6:3-5). It will be further observed that for all the wickedness of the pre-flood world, though some sins are mentioned under general terms such as "violence," no sin is particularly mentioned except this, that men were marrying whomever they chose, and because they saw that the women were beautiful.

I trust that it will not escape the reader that North America is at the same place, namely men are marrying whomever they choose, and in particular, they are seeking the most beautiful ones. Nor is it only unbelievers that are doing as much, but the church too, and that in general. Someone might ask: What is it about choosing one's own wife, that it should be considered so wicked by God? To our minds and culture, it is arranged marriages that are bad, certainly not choosing one's own wife, nor falling in love; and definitely not falling in love with a beautiful woman! The reader is encouraged to ponder this for himself. Yet to assist somewhat, I point the reader's attention to the following observations. First, when a man chooses his own wife, it is rebellion against God's ordained order in marriage. Second, it is rebellion against the authority of one's parents. Third, it is following the flesh - choosing one's own wife, and particularly after observing feminine beauty. Fourth, it causes women to be rejected because of sub-standard physical beauty or defects, thereby making a mockery of the love of Christ for His church, for He died for (ugly) sinners. Fifth, it therefore makes it very difficult for godly women to find a husband, since godly women dress modestly, and so their physical beauty will not be so obvious. Sixth, it therefore promotes indecency and lewd clothing among women in their efforts to attract men to marry them. (Our culture is ample evidence of this). Seventh, it places men in unacceptable positions, forcing them to look for a wife by looking at beautiful women, rather than looking to their parents. Eighth, it therefore leads to fornication, as is also clear from our culture. More things could be said, but to be brief, I pass it by.

There are other examples in the Scriptures of those that rebelled against the practice of arranged marriages. Esau, for example, married two women without consulting his parents. These women "were a grief of mind to Isaac and Rebekah." (Gen 26:35). Consider the case of Jacob, who was sent by his father to take himself a wife from among Laban's daughters. He fell in love with Rachel, yet he ended up marrying four women, to his own displeasure and shame. Nor can it be denied that part of the issue between Jacob and Laban was that Laban intended to give away Leah, but Jacob loved Rachel. (Gen 29). Consider Shechem, who fell in love with Dinah, the daughter of Jacob, and defiled her. However much he tried to follow the proper procedure thereafter, his sin ended up bringing about his death and the destruction of his entire town. (Gen 34) Or consider the example of Judah, who left his family and found himself a wife. His offspring by her were so wicked that the Lord put two of them to death. (See Gen 38). Samson fell in love with Delilah, who was his down fall. (Jud 15). Amnon fell in love with his half-sister, Tamar, and raped her. (2 Sam 13). And even in the case of David's first wife Michal, who had fallen in love with him, the marriage was a source of much grief to David, and in the end Michal despised David and died childless. (2 Sam 6:16,23).

Therefore, in every recorded case where a marriage or a relationship was initiated because someone had fallen in love, the outcome was grief and problems, frequently ending in great sin and personal disaster. It is hard not to make certain conclusions from these obvious historical accounts. But since the Scriptures provide more than histories, it is wise to delay conclusions until the matter has been considered more fully.

More facts may be gleaned from the historical accounts of marriage in the Bible. It will be observed that while the parents had the right and responsibility to find wives for their sons, and to give their daughters in marriage, yet once a man or woman had been married, the responsibility for a second spouse fell on themselves. For example, David was given Michal as his first wife. Yet when it came to his other wives, he found them for himself. Consider the case of David's marriage to Abigail, the widow of Carmel. David simply sent his men with an offer of marriage, and she accepted - of her own volition. (1 Sam 25:39-41). Likewise, Abraham took Hagar to wife of his own volition. But since Hagar was a virgin, she was under the authority of her mistress, and so we read, "And Sarah took Hagar.... and gave her to her husband Abram to be his wife." (Gen 16:3). It will be immediately observed that this is exactly what our text in Corinthians has said, namely that the father has authority over his virgin daughters, to give them in marriage, but the widow has the liberty to marry whomever she will.

It may also be noted from this that when the parents have died, or if they are far away, then the responsibility of arranging the marriage of a young man or virgin woman is given to the authority or guardian of that person. Thus, again, Sarah had the right to give Hagar in marriage. Likewise did Leah and Rachel give their handmaids as wives to Jacob. (Gen 30:3, 9). Similarly, as was pointed out above, Pharaoh took upon himself to find a wife for Joseph, and a later Pharaoh did the same, finding a wife for Hadad. Likewise also did Jehoida the priest find wives for the young king Joash; the king's parents and grandparents being dead. (2 Chron 22-24).

However, if the parents are dead and there is no immediate guardian, then the person is at liberty to marry as they wish. For example, Jeremiah wrote to the few exiles that were carried away to Babylon: "Take ye wives and beget sons and daughters..." (Jer 29:6). And God commanded concerning the daughters of a certain dead man named Zelophehad, "Let them marry to whom they think best...." (Num 36:6).

A review is in order. It has been seen that God established marriage and that He did so by arranging for the marriage of Adam to Eve. It has been seen that from the beginning of time people of all backgrounds have followed this divine institution of marriage, both giving their daughters in marriage and finding wives for their sons. It was noted that the father generally determined the time of the wedding. Further, it has been observed that arranged marriages were not practised by all individuals, but that the few in Scripture who did not were all encompassed by troubles. Even those marriages that the parents did arrange, if it was done so because someone had fallen in love, the marriage was troublesome. And, finally, both the widow and the widower have the right to find their own second spouse.

3. Various Instructions and Comments about Marriage

In the preceding section it was established from Biblical history that arranged marriages were the norm throughout the Middle East from the time of Adam to the time of Christ. In this section, the intent is to examine, not historical accounts, but what the Scriptures specifically teach and say regarding this practice.

In our text before us, in Paul's letter to the Corinthians, we discover that marriage is meant for all, that divorce is non-optional (except in the case of fornication), that fathers have the right to give their daughters in marriage, that the widower has the right to determine when he will marry the virgin that has been betrothed to him, and that a widow, (by marriage freed from the authority of her father and by the death of her husband freed from his authority), is at liberty to marry "whom she will."

What does the rest of Scripture say concerning arranged marriages? In the Old Testament, God gave a command to the Israelites regarding marriage, specifically marriages to foreigners. He said: "Neither shalt thou make marriages with them: thy daughter thou shalt not give unto his son, nor his daughter shalt thou take unto thy son." (Deut 7:3). Although the primary intent of this law is to forbid the Israelites from marrying people who are outside the faith in the one true God, it can be seen that the command takes for granted that they would give their daughters in marriage and find wives for their sons. Indeed, throughout the Law, given by God to Moses, it is continually taken for granted that marriages will be arranged by the parents. For instance, we read, "If his master give him a wife." (Ex 21:4) Or again, "If a man sell his daughter as a maidservant... (she has been) betrothed to (her master)." (Ex 21:7,8). And again, "If he have betrothed her to his son..." (Ex 21:9). Again, "If a man entice a maid that is not betrothed, and lie with her, he shall surely endow her to be his wife. If her father utterly refuse to give her unto him, he shall pay money...." (Ex 22:16). Other similar commands could be set forth.

Let us consider again the message that the prophet Jeremiah gave to the Israelites which were in exile in Babylon: "Take ye wives, and beget sons and daughters, and take wives for your sons, and give your daughters to husbands, that they may bear sons and daughters, that ye may be increased there, and not diminished." (Jer 29:6). To the older men, Jeremiah instructs them to take their own wives. As was pointed out above, this is because either their parents were dead (in the battle with the Babylonians), or they were widowers (their wives died in the battle). Such men are commanded to find themselves a wife, to marry, and to have children. Though they could find their own wives, yet they were commanded to arrange for the marriages of their children: "Take wives for your sons, and give your daughters to husbands." Here God particularly inspired the prophet Jeremiah to command the Israelites to arrange for the marriages of their children. Since it is commanded, we learn that arranged marriages have Divine approval, Divine authority, and that the exiles were left without alternative.

As in the Law, so in the New Testament, the practice of arranged marriages is taken for granted. Jesus Himself made several passing comments about it. First, in the parable of the wedding, Jesus said, "The kingdom of heaven is like unto a certain king, which made a marriage for his son." (Mt 22:2). Second, in that same chapter, Jesus said, "In the resurrection they neither marry nor are given in marriage; but are as the angels of God in heaven." (Mt 22:30). Notice the word, *given*. This word occurs in all three gospels that contain this statement. (See also: Mk 12:25, Lk 20:34,35). Third, Jesus said, "But as the days of Noah were, so shall also the coming of the Son of man be. For as in the days before the flood, they were eating and drinking, marrying and giving in marriage, until the day that Noah entered into the ark." (Mt 24:38).

In all three of these texts Jesus made mention of the practice of being given in marriage. The first was in the context of a spiritual analogy and a future "wedding." We see here, as has been shown before, that the father determines the time of the wedding of his son. The second text informs us that the practice of being given in marriage will cease only at the resurrection. The third text informs us that the custom will stand as historical fact, from Adam until Christ's coming, for it was a pre-flood practice, and shall likewise be at His coming. (See also Lk 17:27-30).

Some would like to say that parental-arranged marriages was only a custom of the past, and that the modern practice common among Christians in the Western world is an equally valid custom. Is it so? What text of Scripture can anyone bring forward to prove that God approves of the current customs? It is usual for the church to find Scripture to back up its practices. Let the defenders of the modern customs attempt it.

As is clear from what has been said, there is ample proof to show God's approval of arranged marriages. But who can find one single verse that teaches a man should look for his own wife, by dating, by courting, by looking for something he likes, or by waiting to fall in love? Indeed, it has already been shown that God considered it a great evil that the men of Noah's generation were marrying whomever they chose. And it has been shown from every example of someone falling in love, that either the marriage was overtly forbidden, or there was much evil in the marriage afterward. It is certain from all that is in the Scriptures, that arranged marriages is a fundamental part of marriage as established by God from the beginning. God established His divine blue-print for marriage when he found a wife for Adam, and gave Eve to him. Such has been practised throughout history, just as marriage has. It has been rejected by some, even as some have dishonoured marriage. The Scriptures categorically assume it to be practised, freely using it in commands and comments, just as freely as marriage is assumed to be practised. And it is irrefutable that it has full approval from God.

4. The Issues of Dowries

On occasion, the Scriptures mention dowries. Webster's dictionary has two definitions for the word *dowry*. First, "The money, goods, or estates which a woman brings to her husband in marriage." And second, "The reward price paid for a wife." The first was common during the Middle Ages. When a wealthy noble, prince or king married a woman, it was expected that she would bring with her a large estate. If she did not have enough wealth with her estate, the woman was not considered as a potential wife. This practice helped to establish an ungodly class division in society, perpetually keeping the kings and princes separate from nobles, and nobles separate from the middle class, and the middle class separate from the poor. But there is no example of this type of a dowry mentioned in Scripture. And as may be seen from the comparison between marriage and Christ and His church, the practice throws things up-side-down. It is not the church that brings a wealthy estate to Christ, but Christ that showers gifts on the church, His bride. And it is surely significant that this inverted practice of dowries in the Middle Ages occurred at the same time that the Roman Catholic church sank into the damnable errors of salvation by works, rather than by faith in Christ.

The second definition, and quite to the contrary, refers to the price that a man would pay to a woman's father to obtain her for his wife. This is found multiple times in the Scriptures.

However, it appears that originally there was no dowry required when the marriage was arranged by the parents. No mention of a dowry is made in the account of the first wedding, between Adam and Eve. Nor, when Abraham's servant asked for Rebekah as a wife for Isaac is any mention whatsoever made of a dowry. However, after the marriage was agreed on, the servant lavished Rebekah and her family liberally with gifts, in accordance with the wealth of Abraham.

Sometimes, for so we observe in the Scriptures, a man would offer his daughter to anyone that would perform a great feat. Caleb did this, saying, "He that smiteth Kirjathsepher, and that taketh it, to him will I give Achsah my daughter to wife." (Jud 1:12). This might be worse than it sounds, except for the fact that Caleb knew he was only speaking to Israelites, and that they were presently in the process of carrying out God's commands of conquering Canaan. Therefore, Caleb was hardly doing anything beyond saying he would give his daughter to a man with great faith in God. In any case, no dowry of money was required.

But the case is quite different when someone was in love and tried to obtain a wife. For example, when Laban invited Jacob to name his wages for his work, he voluntarily responded: "I will serve thee seven years for Rachel thy younger daughter." (Gen 29:18). And Laban accepted. Likewise, we read that when Shechem tried to obtain Dinah for his wife, he said to Jacob her father, "Ask me never so much dowry and gift, and I will give according as ye say unto me." (Gen 34:12). Both of these accounts concern a man that was greatly in love with the woman he was trying to obtain as a wife, and both set of their own volition an enormously high value on the woman. Jacob's "wage," to put it into perspective, amounts to at least $140,000.00, assuming he was only earning $20,000 per year! And Shechem was so bold, or shall I say so crazed, that he put no limit whatsoever on the dowry.

Similarly, the Law makes mention of a dowry only when an arranged marriage is **not** followed. Moses writes, "And if a man entice a maid that is not betrothed, and lie with her, he shall surely endow her to be his wife. If her father utterly refuse to give her unto him, he shall pay money according to the dowry of virgins." (Ex 22:17). In the parallel passage, when this law is repeated, we are told the amount of this dowry: "If a man find a damsel that is a virgin, which is not betrothed, and lay hold on her, and lie with her, and they be found; then the man that lay with her shall give unto the damsel's father fifty shekels of silver and she shall be his wife: because he hath humbled her, he may not put her away all his days." (Deut. 22:28,229). This is the only mention in the Law about a dowry. Therefore, this 50 shekels of silver was not so much a dowry, as a penalty imposed on the man for violating the woman, and for rebelling against God's plan of arranged marriages. Indeed, in setting the penalty at this figure, God was testifying that the crime was equal to the man's life, for the "estimation" of a healthy young male was also 50 shekels of silver. (see: Lev 27:3).

Incidentally, it is worth noting that this law only applied if the woman was a virgin, and if she was not betrothed yet. In other words, both the man and the woman he seduced had come of age without their parents finding a spouse for them. The command in our text in Corinthians comes to mind: "To avoid fornication, let every man have his own wife, and let every woman have her own husband." If the parents had been more diligent in finding spouses for either of these two, the sorry event would likely have never happened. And it is surely with this parental failure in mind that the Lord graciously allows the man to live, though death was the usual penalty for most sexual sins. Indeed, his death is intimated by making the penalty equal to his life's estimation. And it surely with this parental failure in mind that the Lord also graciously commands the man to marry the woman, as without this provision, she would have been destitute, forsaken in the community, and would quite likely have become a single-mom. The reader is encouraged to reflect on the wisdom and justice of commanding the man to marry the woman he seduced, for although it is generally abhorred today, it was common among Christian communities as little as 75 years ago.

One more example is in order, namely that of the marriage of David and Michal. David felt that he was too poor a man to possibly afford a dowry for a king's daughter. The crafty king took advantage of this, and the fact that his second daughter, Michal, had fallen in love with David, saying, "The king desireth not any dowry, but an hundred foreskins of the Philistines." (1 Sam 18:17-25). So here again, we have a dowry named when there was love involved, and when one was attempting to obtain someone else's hand in marriage. It is surely a sad thing that David did not see through this, for not only was king Saul being deceitful (he was trying to have David killed in attempting the dowry), but to obtain the dowry David had to stain his belt with blood shed during peace time as if in war. Furthermore, the marriage aggravated Saul's disposition against David, Michal was eventually given to another man, only to return to David much later, despise him, and die childless.

In conclusion, when the Lord instituted marriage, no mention was made of dowries, nor was any command specifically given about it. A man could, according to his ability, shower his bride and the brides family with gifts, to show his liberality and his appreciation for his wife. Indeed, did not Christ shower the church, His bride, with gifts from above? The custom of dowries originally came into effect only when men sought to obtain for themselves a woman that they were in love with. It is quite possible that from this restricted beginning, the custom eventually spread and became much more common, even for arranged marriages. And many hundreds of years later it even became inverted in some places, so that the woman brought a dowry with her to the man.

5. Abuses in Arranged Marriages

"And God looked upon the earth, and behold it was corrupt, for all flesh had corrupted his way upon the earth." (Gen 6:12). So said God about the pre-flood people. And with such a record, it is no surprise that man should also corrupt, not only the beautiful thing of marriage, but also the wonderful practice of arranged marriages. Since arranged marriages are viewed so negatively by the West, it is valuable to mention some of its abuses, so that the pure integrity of God's original may shine the brighter.

One abuse is to arrange a marriage to obtain wealth. One may readily see, that if a dowry is introduced into the practice, then daughters become valuable assets that may be sold for lucrative profits. Jacob volunteered to serve Laban seven years to obtain Rachel. But Laban turned it around, and after deceitfully giving Leah instead, he then demanded Jacob, saying: "Fulfil her week, and we will give thee [Rachel] also, for the service which thou shall serve with me yet seven other years." (Gen 29:27). Nor did this wickedness go unnoticed, for Laban's own daughters concluded, saying, "Are we not counted of him as strangers? For he has sold us, and hath quite devoured also our money." (Gen 31:15). Their evident dislike for what Laban did to them is proof that dowries were uncommon in those days. Nor is it surprising that Laban should abuse marriage this way, for it is evident from the way that he dealt with Jacob that he was a deceitful liar, always trying to make more money. (See: Gen 31:41). Sadly, history is replete with many other examples of people that have tried to make money by selling off their daughters.

Another abuse of arranged marriages is to use it as a means of managing relations with other countries. For example, King Solomon married the daughter of Pharaoh to "make affinity with Egypt." (1 King 3:1). This marriage does not seem to have been arranged - certainly not by Solomon's father, David. Yet it demonstrates what an abuse of life it is to use marriage as a means of obtaining political peace. Sadly, it also demonstrates how fruitless such a practise is. Indeed, Solomon's intentions failed him completely, for no sooner had he died than Egypt attacked Jerusalem - bringing a tragic end to the peaceful relations that had existed between Israel and Egypt since the Exodus. (1 Kings 14:25,26).

A second example of this abuse is king Jehoshaphat. After about 70 years of war and unrest between Judah and Israel, Jehoshaphat became king of Judah. Of him it says, "He made peace with the king of Israel." (1 King 22:44). And how did this man bring about this peace? "He joined affinity with Ahab" the king of Israel by taking a daughter of Ahab as a wife for his son. (2 Chr 18:1, 21:1-6). But the affinity by marriage was no more successful than Solomon's with Egypt. In fact, it gained Jehoshaphat nothing but trouble in his own life, solved none of the issues separating Judah and Israel, and served only to bring the wicked practices of Ahab into the kingdom of Judah. Sadly, history is replete with many similar examples of kings attempting to make alliances with other nations by arranging for marriages of princes with princesses of the other kingdoms.

In both of the above abuses, the parents used their power to arrange a marriage for their own profit, without the least concern for their son or daughter. And so it is that any time a parent seeks to arrange a marriage without due consideration for the spiritual well-being of their children, it is an abuse of marriage. God found a wife for Adam because He recognized that "it was not good for the man to be alone." And God chose Eve for Adam because she "was an help meet for him." So we see that in God's divine example, the marriage was arranged solely with the interest of the two children in mind. Now if God, who does whatever He pleases in heaven and earth, did as much, how much more should parents seek only the well-being of their children when they arrange their marriages?

The Scriptures testify that the Israelites sometimes took pagan daughters for their sons, and gave their daughters to pagan sons. (see: Jud 3:5,6, Neh 13:23-25). This is also a serious abuse of arranged marriages, for, as was seen above, God's people were expressly forbidden from doing so. (Deut 7:3). But it is also a serious abuse of arranged marriages because it shows complete disregard for the spiritual well-being of the children. Indeed, this is the very reason why God forbids such marriages, saying, "For they will turn away thy son from following me, that they may serve other gods." (Deut 7:4). No more proof of this is needed than the tragic example of king Solomon, and how his wives turned him away from God to serve idols. (1 Kin 11:4, Neh 13:26).

6. Marriage compared to Christ and His church

Is the modern reader still sceptical about arranged marriages? There is one more proof that God has given us in the Scriptures, and this distinctly gives the final blow to any contrary arguments. We have seen that Christ began a certain parable by saying, "The kingdom of heaven is like unto a certain king, which made a marriage for his son." (Mt 22:2). The parable was particularly about how the invited guests rejected the invitation to come to this great wedding, and how the father then directed his servants to invite others. Nevertheless, it is certain from all of Scripture that the great spiritual truths of Christianity are "like" a marriage. Thus, for example, we read, "As a young man rejoiceth over the bride, so shall thy God rejoice over thee." (Isa 62:5) Incidently, it will be noted that arranged marriages are not sour or sorrowful, as so many people try to depict them today. No, and much to the contrary, here God expressly states that the young man rejoices over his bride! But my point is that the Holy Spirit here compares the joy of marriage with the joy that God has over His people.

As was mentioned in a previous chapter, God spoke to the prophet Hosea, saying, "Go yet love a woman beloved of her friend, yet an adulteress, according to the love of God toward the children of Israel, who look to other gods..." (Hos 3:1) Here the prophet affirms how horrible adultery is, how revolting it is to the faithful spouse, and how unnatural it is for love to remain in the marriage after this. But the spiritual truths are hereby also confirmed, namely that to worship anyone or anything other than the one true God, and to do so in any other way than He has commanded, is spiritual adultery, and horribly grievous to God. And the enormous, great, patient, and tender love of God for His poor straying children is also affirmed.

The comparisons are more common, and much more bold in the New Testament. For example, in the letter to the Romans, the law that binds one in marriage until the death of a spouse is used to illustrate how Christ set us free from the law. In this regard, the Holy Spirit testifies, saying,

> For the woman which hath an husband is bound by the law to her husband so long as he liveth: but if the husband be dead, she is loosed from the law of her husband.... Wherefore, my brethren, ye also are become dead to the law by the body of Christ; that ye should be married to another, even to him who is raised from the dead, that we should bring forth fruit to God.
>
> (Rom 7:2-4).

Here the apostle affirms that marriage is for life, that a widow may remarry, and that one main purpose of marriage is to produce godly offspring. And from these principles of marriage he affirms the similar spiritual truths that if it were not for Christ all men would be sunk to hell by their transgression of the law, being bound to it irreversibly. But he also affirms that by Christ's death we are freed from the binding power of God's law, and that one main purpose of this is to produce the fruit of godliness.

In another passage, the apostle Paul says to the Corinthian church, "I espoused you to one husband, that I may present you as a chaste virgin to Christ." (2 Cor 11:2). The apostle here affirms that fornication is sin, and that remaining a virgin until married is what the righteousness of God requires. But he also affirms the right of a father to betroth his daughter in marriage. All of this he does incidently, by using marriage as a comparison of the spiritual truths of the believer. In particular the apostle affirms the spiritual truths that the Christian is to have one head, one husband, even Christ; that while on the earth we live as if we are "espoused" - called His wife, and He our husband, but waiting for the "marriage supper of the Lamb." (Rev 19:7). Further, the truth is affirmed that Christians are to worship Christ alone, never idols or wealth. (1 Cor 10:21, Col 3:1-5).

Again, in another beautiful and magnificent passage, the Holy Spirit testifies to the likeness between marriage and Christ's church, saying,

> Wives, submit yourselves unto your own husbands, as unto the Lord. For the husband is the head of the wife, even as Christ is the head of the church; and he is the saviour of the body. Therefore, as the church is subject to Christ, let the wives be to their own husbands in every thing. Husbands, love your wives, even as Christ also loved the church and gave himself up for it: That he might sanctify and cleanse it... that he might present it to himself a glorious church, not having spot or wrinkle.... but that it should be holy.... So ought men to love their wives, as their own bodies... For we are members of his body, of his flesh, and of his bones. For this cause shall a man leave his father and mother, and shall be joined unto his wife, and they two shall be one flesh. This is a great mystery; but I speak concerning Christ and the church.
>
> (Eph 5:22-32)

Here many truths about marriage are affirmed, namely that the wife is to submit to her husband, the husband is to love his wife more than his own life, the marriage bond is until death, that God unites the two people into one flesh, that the marriage bed is to be kept pure, and that marriage is a great mystery. And by each and every one of these truths, the apostle affirms the similar spiritual truth in the church, namely that the church has Christ as her husband, that the church is to submit to Christ, that Christ loved the church with an unfathomable love, even to His own death for her, that God makes believers one flesh with Christ, that the church and her relationship to Christ is a great mystery.

Further, the Scriptures testify of the hand of the Father in choosing a bride for His Son. Jesus Himself testifies, saying, "All that the Father giveth to me will come to me, and him that cometh to me I will in no wise cast out." (Jn 6:37) And again, "And this is the Father's will which hath sent me, that of all which he hath given me I should lose nothing, but should raise it up again at the last day." (Jn 6:39). And again, "No man can come unto me, except the Father which hath sent me draw him." (Jn 6:44). And again, "Every man therefore that hath heard, and hath learned of the Father, cometh unto me." (Jn 6:45). And again, "My Father which gave them to me is greater than all; and no man is able to pluck them out of my Father's hand." (Jn 10:29). And again, "Herein is my Father glorified, that ye bear much fruit; so shall ye be my disciples." (Jn 15:8). And again, "Thou hast given Thy son power over all flesh that he should give eternal life to as many as thou hast given him." (Jn 17:1). And again, "I have manifested Thy name unto the men which Thou gavest me out of the world: Thine they were, and thou gavest them to me..." (Jn 17:6). And again, "Father, I will that they also, whom thou hast given me, be with me where I am...." (Jn 17:24). No less than nine times, Jesus tells us that believers are those that the Father gave Him.

Nor does Christ alone testify to these things, for the apostle Peter writes "to the strangers.... to the Elect according to the foreknowledge of God the Father..." And the apostle Paul writes, "Therefore, as the elect of God, put on... kindness, humbleness of mind, meekness.... forgiving one another .... even as Christ forgave you." (Col 3:12,13). And again, Paul writes, "Knowing, brethren beloved, your election of God." (1 Thes 1:4). And again, "according to the faith of God's elect." (Titus 1:1).

It is irrefutable by these numerous statements, that the church, the bride of Christ, consists of those that were given to Christ by the Father. Here is affirmed the beauty of arranged marriages, namely the father finding a spouse for his son, the son rejoicing in the gift from the father, and the son loving the wife unconditionally. But see how these beautiful and glorious truths are distorted, even demolished by the practices so common among churches in the West? For when a man finds his own wife, he of necessity looks for those things he likes, he of necessity seeks his own profit, he of necessity looks, at least partially, for physical beauty. And the great truths of Christ's love, of the Father's gift, of Christ receiving unconditionally every one that the Father gives him (no matter how "ugly" they may be), of our humility and His glory, and of our eternal life only in Him, are lost, distorted and contorted out of measure.

Finally, it will be pointed out that one of the great truths about the return of Christ, is that the Father has set the date. "But of that day, and that hour, knoweth no man, no, nor the angels which are in heaven, nether the Son, but the Father." (Mk 13:32). Therefore not even Christ knows when this day is. Now, since the return of Christ is compared in Scripture to a wedding, and to a groom coming for his bride, we see again that it is the Father that sets the time of the wedding, even as we have learned of arranged marriages from the Scripture.

In conclusion, then, the spiritual truths of Christ and His church are found to affirm the laws of marriage. And similarly, the practices and laws of marriage affirm the spiritual truths of Christ and His church. Moreover, the historical examples of marriages in the Bible affirm both the spiritual and the physical truths, for while God's prophets are urged to love their adulterous wives to show the matchless love of God for his people, on the other hand, every marriage that was initiated because someone had fallen in love ended in grief and personal disaster. Further, marriage was instituted by none other than God Himself, who noted Adam's need, and brought him a wife that was able to help him. And finally, the Scriptures everywhere commend or command arranged marriages. Can anyone possibly deny, after all this testimony and comparison, that God intended marriage so to be? He were foolish to attempt it. And if the reader try, he will soon discover there is not a drop of commendation in the Scripture to support the modern practice of a man choosing his own wife, or of people waiting to fall in love before they marry. Let the reader ponder all these things.

7. Practical Applications

It would be short-sighted not to end this chapter with at least several practical applications from the Scriptures.

First, is the reader a parent? Then take up this godly practice that has too long been buried in derision. It is your privilege and responsibility to give your daughters in marriage and to find wives for your sons.

Second, is the reader single? Then reject the idea of finding your own partner. Rather, submit to the Lord's way and timing. Learn to honour your parents and to obey them, by asking them to find you a spouse, as is their responsibility. And help them to understand the importance of finding a spouse that is a believer.

Third, parents are urged to seek the Lord's help in this most awesome responsibility. A bad marriage is devastating. Solomon wrote several proverbs that drive this point home. For example, "A virtuous woman is a crown to her husband, but she that maketh ashamed is as rottenness in his bones." (Pr 12:4). Again, it says, "It is better to dwell in a corner of the housetop, than with a brawling woman in a wide house." (Pr 21:9). When one compares this to the potential blessing of a godly wife as found in the last chapter of Proverbs, the contrast is drastic. Be alert to this, and take your responsibility with the utmost seriousness. Pray! Furthermore, the Scriptures declare, "Houses and riches are the inheritance of fathers: and a prudent wife is from the Lord." (Pr 19:14). Finding a wife for one's son is not as easy as giving him an inheritance. And notice that no matter what you do, or what your involvement, if a man marries a prudent wife, the Lord takes all the credit. Therefore, seek the Lord's help; He can give it and you need it badly. Seek the Lord's face and His timing, even as Abraham's servant did - to his joy and success. (See Gen 24).

Fourth, the reader is specifically urged not to be deceived by the emotion of love. God has put certain restraints on who is permitted to marry who. Do not allow "love" to over-rule God's constraints. As was shown above, there are multiple examples in the Scriptures of those who allowed falling in love to direct their marriages; but always to their own trouble or destruction. The reader is reminded of Samson, who fell in love twice, both times to Philistine women. (See Jud 14:1-7, 16:4,5). Although the word of God expressly forbade such a marriage, Samson acted on his emotions, for he had "fallen in love." He brought disaster to himself. And remember David's son Amnon, who fell in love with his half-sister, Tamar. Although God's word forbids a man from marrying his sister, Amnon allowed love to guide him until it brought evil, hate, pain, and death to himself, and ruin to his sister. Therefore, banish the idea that falling in love is proof of God's direction. It is no such thing. In fact, as has been shown, it is very likely in direct contradiction to God's will.

Fifth remember the counsel: "Stir not up, nor awake love until he please." (Songs 2:7). This word of caution is repeated no less than three times in that short book. (See also 3:5, 8:4). Indeed, Amnon's tragedy may have been fresh in Solomon's mind when he penned those words. Why is such a warning necessary? Consider the power of love. Solomon wrote:

> Love is strong as death, jealousy is cruel as the grave. The coals thereof are coals of fire, which has a most vehement flame. Many waters cannot quench love, neither can the floods drown it. If a man would give all the substance of his house for love, it would utterly be contemned.
>
> (Songs 8:6,7).

Notice that both Amnon and Samson were consumed by their love, until they did exactly this: they gave all the wealth of their lives! Samson scorned even the strength of the Holy Spirit within him, and gave it up in wickedness because he was carried to folly by the flame of love that had engulfed him. Both men were destroyed by that unquenchable, blazing fire. "Can a man take fire in his bosom, and his clothes not be burned?" (Pr 6:27). So it was with these men. So then, love is not a game, nor something to be experimented with before marriage. It is most serious. It is most beautiful in marriage, but before or outside of marriage it is disastrous. So then, beware of following the world's paths to marriage and so arousing love toward one that the Lord does not want you to marry. Therefore, honour marriage and encourage the godly path rather than the world's, for "whosoever findeth a wife findeth a good thing, and obtaineth favor of the Lord." (Pr 18:22).

Sixth, and lastly, the reader is encouraged to a simple examination of the outcome of the practices of our day, in order to point him back to God's original will. The church has followed the world's ways of finding a spouse. And what is the outcome? Fornication, rape, adultery, broken marriages, divorce, lewd clothing, lust, and an abundance of single people. These tragedies are in the church, and in numbers that should make us tremble. As the pre-flood "sons of God," and as Esau, Judah, Shechem, Samson, and Amnon all brought grief, tragedy, and death by their practices, the same is happening today. Let us repent of our foolishness and sinful customs, and let us return to the Lord. He is a forgiving and merciful God and He can heal us.

In conclusion, then, the Scriptures teach that all should marry, and it is expected that they marry young. But in contrast, most Western churches today feel that God calls many people to remain single, and that marriage is best postponed until both the man and woman are well educated and established in their careers.

The Scriptures teach that divorce is not an option for the Christian, and that remarriage is forbidden. But in contrast, many today almost freely divorce and remarry.

The Scriptures teach that older widows and widowers should be devoted in body and spirit to the Lord, caring for what pleases Him, and giving themselves to prayer and fasting. And the Scriptures loudly rebuke the widow that lives in pleasure. But in stark contrast, most churches encourage people to save up a huge retirement fund, so that they can spend their last days in luxury and pleasure, travelling the world.

The Scriptures teach that some widowers should remarry, and that it is not sin for such a man to marry a young woman. But in contrast, the world and the church downplay this, and view it almost with abhorrence, insulting the man.

The Scriptures teach that parents should find wives for their sons, and give their daughters in marriage. But most churches in the West view this as an absurd custom of an uneducated and poorly-evolved people of the past. And they view it as cause of poverty, suicide, domestic abuse, and unhappy marriages in the East.[5]

The Scriptures teach that parents should find spouses for their children. But in contrast, young men are encouraged to find their own wives by spending time with young women, and by falling in love with one of them.

The Scriptures teach that husbands are the head of the wife. But many in the West think this is appalling and disgraceful.

Let the reader carefully consider these things, for it is undisputable that churches in North America have strayed far from the truths of Scriptural Marriage. The salt has lost is savour. And the world is rushing head long into corruption as a result. "But Noah found grace in the eyes of the Lord... Noah was a just man and perfect in his generations, and Noah walked with God." (Gen 6:8,9). Let us imitate this man's noble faith and actions, that we be not condemned with the world. And let us, by faith in God and His word, have the courage to practice "Scriptural Marriage."

---

5   Does the reader doubt that many in the West feel this way? One only need read the Winter 2008/2009 issue of "Child View," a publication of World Vision Canada, in which arranged marriages in Afghanistan are accused of these very things, and where they tell the reader they are striving to stop these things by setting up children's clubs to "teach children of their rights."

Appendix A
Historical Considerations: Church and Marriage

The practice of arranged marriages is virtually unheard of today in the West. What happened? How is it that the church ceased to practice arranged marriages? Or, did the church ever really practice such a thing? In view of these real and important questions, it is necessary, in this appendix, to consider the history of the church as it relates to arranged marriages.

It was shown from the Scriptures that arranged marriages were the norm throughout the known world from the time of Adam to the time of Christ. The practice remained a world-wide norm right up until the time of the Reformation. But shortly thereafter the practise fell by the way side in European countries. Let us consider how this came about.

By the power of God the good news of Jesus Christ successfully spread and conquered most of the Middle East, Rome, and Europe by the end of the sixth century. With the fall of Rome (circa 476 AD), Western Europe fell into what is called the Medieval period. By the time the year 1500 rolled around, all of Europe, including England, Spain, France, Germany, Switzerland, Scotland, and the Netherlands, was essentially one big "Christian" community. To be sure there was plenty of rivalry, wars, national uprisings, and conflicts. There was also perpetual struggles within the church, particularly concerning the Pope. But however many divisions there were, the reality is that there was a reasonably uniform culture and society across all these lands and peoples. It is not that much unlike the fact that today there is still a uniformity of culture in Europe and North America, in spite of a multitude of religious and national distinctions. In the 1500's however, the power and presence of the church was fundamental to the core of society and all its common customs and laws. This fact had a huge influence on the Reformation, and the fears and wars that ensued because of it. Some people, such as Erasmus, (1466-1536), the famous scholar of Rotterdam, abandoned the Reformation because of a fear of "rending the seamless robe of Christ," as he and others put it. They could not bear to see the European church divided.

Like most societies in history, the church-society of the early 1500's was traditional. In fact, many of the debates between Reformers and the Roman Catholics hinged on whether the Reformers could prove from church history that their doctrines were **not** new. Consequently, books of that era often contain many references to what the church "Fathers" had said on this or that issue - to prove that nothing new was being put forward. Whatever errors and changes were in the church at that time, they had surely come in slowly and subtly over many years.

It is safe to conclude from all of this that marriage customs would have changed very little between the time of the apostles and the beginning of the Reformation. Indeed, other than the important and divisive issue of the marriage of clergy in the church, both the Reformers and the Catholics generally agreed on matters of marriage, and both practised arranged marriages.

I provide the reader with a few particular examples to verify these things. We begin with European kings, and their children. In England, for instance, king Henry VII, (1456-1509), betrothed three of his children, each in an attempt to create political alliances. He arranged the marriage of his son Arthur to princess Katharine to create an alliance with her father, the king of Aragon. He arranged the marriage of his daughter Margaret with James V of Scotland, to secure an alliance with them. And when Arthur died early, the desperate king chose to keep the alliance by betrothing the widow Katharine, to his other son, Henry. At the time of the betrothal, Henry (the famous Henry VIII, 1491-1547) was still a boy. The marriage took place years later, when Henry was 18.

Things were similar in Scotland. For instance, in 1548 Mary, afterwards called "Queen of Scots," was first betrothed to Edward VI, of England, while both were young. Yet the Scottish parliament and nobility changed their minds, and later betrothed her to the Dauphin (Francis II, king of France) when she was but five. She married him at the age of 15.

Nor were things different on the Continent. Consider, for instance, William, Prince of Orange, (1533-1584). Though raised in a God-fearing home of Lutheran persuasion, from the age of 11 he was educated in a Roman Catholic court under the Emperor, Charles V. When William was still quite young, Emperor Charles chose a wife for him, namely Anne, heiress of the Count of Buren. They were married when William was 18. As Anne did not live very long, William took a second wife, this time choosing for himself, one Anna, niece of the Elector of Saxony. And it is hard to deny that he was seeking by this marriage to develop military alliances with the Lutheran and Calvinistic princes of Germany.

Many other examples could be named, for in the late fifteenth century, it was the undisputed practice of kings and nobles to find wives for their sons and to give their daughters in marriage. Frequently, even, the arrangements were made by Parliament. And as the political tensions between the various kings of Europe was a perpetual concern, these betrothals were frequently used in (mostly vain) attempts to establish peaceful relations with neighbouring countries.

Turning from the realm of princes and princesses, let us consider the practices of the Reformers. Martin Luther (1483-1546), the great Reformer of Germany, was a monk in the Roman Catholic church, and so was forbidden from marriage. Yet as the Reformation progressed, and as Luther studied the Scriptures more, it became painfully obvious that the idea of a celibate clergy was a tragic innovation in the church. In consequence, when nuns defected from their convents, Luther took it upon himself to arrange their marriages. Indeed, he ended up marrying one himself. His biographer, describes Luther's views on arranged marriages:

> The whole institution of marriage was set by Luther within the framework of family relationships. There was no room left for the exercise of unbridled individualism. Matings should be made by families; and whereas parents should not force children to repulsive unions, children in turn should not, because of infatuations, resist reasonable choices on the part of their elders. This whole picture was carried directly over from the Middle Ages, in which Catholic sacramentalism and agrarian society tended to make of marriage an institution for the perpetuation of families and preservation of

properties. The romantic revolution of the Courts of Love in France was at first extramatrimonial, and the combination of romance and marriage was first effected only during the Renaissance." [6]

The author of this quote, Roland Bainton, was opposed to the concept of arranged marriages, as is clear from this and other things he wrote in the same book. Nevertheless, it is clear that Bainton concurs with what has been affirmed above, namely that arranged marriages were the norm throughout the Middle Ages. What Bainton seems to miss, however, is that arranged marriages did not begin with the Middles Ages, but can be traced all the way back to Adam and Eve, as has been shown in chapter seven of this book.

It is also worthwhile noting that the switch to the modern customs began only "during the Renaissance." Bainton would have been more correct to say the change was first effected **by** the Renaissance, though such may certainly be implied by his quote. The Reformation had no interest in changing the God-honoured traditions of arranged marriages. However, the Renaissance, with its emphasis on human achievement, human thought, ancient (pagan) philosophy, and art, rejected true religion. In consequence, it rapidly evolved a new form of marriage, namely a combination of "romance and marriage," as Bainton here words it. It is of particular interest to observe Bainton's reason for the change, namely that in the French courts men gave up having affairs and decided to marry their mistress in the first place. The reader, possibly unfamiliar with life in the Middle Ages, may not be aware that most of the kings and nobles of that time period had mistresses in other countries, and that they would make use of them during their travels. The wicked practice was also common among bishops and popes alike. Europe, in consequence, had a perpetual stream of "bastards," as everyone called the offspring of these "extramatrimonial" affairs.

Nor may one blame arranged marriages for all these affairs. The problem in the church was the celibate clergy and single nuns. And in the public realm, the problem was people that professed to be Christians, but lacked true conversion and regeneration. This, in deed, is what the Reformation was all about: the Catholic church had produced a useless system of works, devoid of lively faith and holy living.

It is also observed from this quote that the change was more than simply how one obtains a wife, but encompassed all that marriage was, whether within

---

6   *Here I Stand: A Life of Martin Luther*, by RH Bainton, c 1978, pgs 233, 234

the family, within the church, or within society. Children were thereby taught to disregard the wishes of their parents. Young people were thought to think in terms of sexual pleasures rather than raising a family. People learned to think of themselves alone, being individualistic. I trust the reader will easily concur that this is in fact where all the Western societies now are. But it was not always this way. And the change was not effected by the Christian church, but by the humanists, by the "Courts of Love," by the wicked and adulterous men that had their mistresses all over the land. And it is surely no surprise that the movement began in France, for that is the only European country that successfully eliminated the Reformed church. And this France did by murdering all the followers of the Reformation.

It is most interesting, in observing history, that the Reformation and the Renaissance happened simultaneously. Both had early beginnings in the late 1400's, both blossomed in the 1500's, and both matured in the 1600's. The effect of these two momentous revolutions happening side by side caused an enormous change in society, and 1500 is usually marked as the end of the Medieval period and the beginning of the Modern period. Or, it is possibly more correct to say that the enormous changes in society produced and allowed these two revolutions. For indeed, about this same time period, Constantinople fell, (in 1453, bringing the Greek new testament to Europe); the cannon and pistol became popular, (putting an end to the power of the nobility and the security of castles); and the printing press was invented, (allowing ideas to be delivered to the masses). Whichever is more correct to say, the reality is that the Reformation and the Renaissance occurred at the same time as huge shifts in society. In the early stages, while it was not perfectly clear which direction these two ships were heading, some men like Erasmus, (who was overtly a humanist, and therefore with the Renaissance), at first fully supported Luther and the Reformation, but then withdrew and clashed with it.

The point is this, namely that these significant changes, and particularly the revival of humanistic thinking and ideologies, eventually effected enormous changes in society and their customs. And sadly, over the space of the next few hundred years, the practice of arranged marriages virtually disappeared from European soil.

Strangely, the church, instead of holding to the teachings of the word of God, allowed the humanists and the Renaissance to sway their thinking. And they all too quickly swallowed this new form of marriage. By the early 1700's, there does not even appear to be the thought of it among the English clergy.

For instance, John Wesley (1703-1791), the famous evangelist of London, was eager to marry. And since he was a young, eligible, wealthy bachelor of great influence, many young women were eager to marry him. His own followers advised that it would be better for his ministry if he would marry, and free himself from all these women followers. When he first found himself a woman that he was willing to marry, his brother dissuaded him because she was of a lower class. By the time Wesley finally found himself another, he was already 48 years old. The woman he married was a widow by the name of Mary Vazeille. His marriage turned out to be a disaster. The two separated after only 15 years of marriage, and Wesley's wife died without him even hearing about it for some time thereafter. In all of this there is not a hint of anyone seeking or practising arranged marriages.

Yet most customs linger to some extent, and even to this present day, there are remnants of the practice of arranged marriages in our modern society. Surely God leaves such things as a testimony to the truth, even as God inspired Moses to teach the Israelites a song that would testify against them after they departed from Him. (Deut 32). Do not most Christian wedding ceremonies ask that important initial question: "Who gives this woman to be married to this man?" And does not the father respond:, "Her mother and I do"? Given the way most people find their spouse, and the attitudes between children and their parents, it is certain that this question is mostly a farce today. Where then did this question come from? It is a testimony to the fact that in the not-that-distant past, marriages were arranged by the parents, and fathers did really give their daughters in marriage.

Moreover, it is common, at least among some of the more conservative Christian groups, for a young man to ask parents for permission to marry their daughter. The practise is hardly more than a formality today, even in Conservative circles, though some times a father will attempt to stop a marriage if he is not pleased with it. But what this "old-fashioned" custom testifies to is the old and ancient practice of arranged marriages, where the parents had the authority over their daughters, and could give them in marriage to whom they chose.

Further, it will be pointed out that while the Western world has generally forsaken arranged marriages, the Eastern world, at least in some places, has retained it. In Afghanistan, for instance, it is estimated that about 80 percent of all marriages are arranged by the parents. India has similarly kept the tradition of arranged marriages. And it is not that unusual to hear of such things in other Eastern countries.

Returning to the matter of church history, it is interesting to note that in the 500 years since the Reformation the conflict between the humanists of the Renaissance and the Christians of the Reformation has pulled and pushed back and forth. At one time the Biblical principles of the Reformation have predominated, at another time the principles of the Renaissance have taken the lead in society. The great revivals of the 1700's and 1800's, brought true religion back, and the principles of the Reformation again dominated. But in the late 1800's, the humanists took a decided lead in the battle by a general acceptance of the theory of evolution and through the idea of higher criticism.[7] The famous preacher C.H. Spurgeon lived during the days when these two false ideas were introduced into Christendom, and he vigorously refuted both. The reader is encouraged to read *The Down Grade Controversy*, (published by Pilgrim Publications), which contains a most interesting summary of what Spurgeon wrote against these two anti-Christian theories.

For over 100 years, now, evolution and higher criticism have dominated both church and society in North America and Europe. The results are obvious. We have gone from societies in which nearly everyone claimed to be a Christian, to now, where people claiming to be Christians are a small minority.

In the past 50 years, the West has seen a change in society that makes the changes of the 1500's pale in comparison. They saw the printing press invented; we have seen the computer and the Internet. They saw the cannon and the pistol come into use; we have seen nuclear war and supersonic airplanes. They saw the revival of man in art and learning in the Renaissance; we have seen an explosion in education, and the man-centred ideology of evolution. They saw the spiritual revival in the Reformation, but we have, sadly, had no parallel in our generation.

---

7   Higher Criticism is the idea that we should study the Bible as any other ancient book. In other words, the idea is that we may learn much from its pages, but we must take everything with a grain of salt because the writers did not have all the facts, and because we (with more science, knowledge and experience) are in a "higher" place of vision and are therefore able to critique the Bible.

BIBLIOGRAPHY

"Strong's Exhaustive Concordance of the Bible," by James Strong, c 1890

"The Analytical Greek Lexicon Revised," by Harold Moulton, c 1977, Zondervan.

"The Reformation in Scotland," by John Knox, Banner of Truth Trust, reprinted from a 1898 edition. Written by the great Reformer, Knox, himself, but put into modern English and spelling to make it readable. It is a superb overview of the reformation of the church in Scotland.

"High School History of England and Canada" by Buckley and Robertson, 1891. This little book provides a quick and excellent overview of the history of England, providing numerous examples of arranged marriages, and of attempts by governments to secure political alliances thereby. But the book is somewhat biased against true Christianity.

"The History of the Reformation," by J. H. Merle D'aubigne, 1872, reprinted by Powder Springs Press. This is a large and somewhat exhaustive book, but it covers only twenty years: 1510 to 1530. The author thoroughly covers these decisive years in every country where the Reformation first occurred: England, Germany, Switzerland, France, and to some extent Italy.

"William the Silent, Prince of Orange," by C.V. Wedgewood, 1944, Yale University Press. In spite of the fact that the author is overtly antagonistic towards Calvinists, (Prince William eventually became one), the book provides fantastic insight into this unique prince that stands far above any of his contemporaries in his concern for his people and his persistence in doing what was right.

"Here I Stand: A Life of Martin Luther," by R. H. Bainton, 1978, Abingdon Press. This is an excellent introductory biography about Luther. The author is evidently a great admirer of Luther, though differs from him on many notable points.

"Robert Murray McCheyne," by Andrew Bonar, 1844, reprinted in 1997 by BPC Paperbacks Ltd. Bonar was a close friend of McCheyne, and so qualified to write this short and interesting biography. The book contains many great insights on McCheyne's pursuit of a holy walk with God, and is inspiring. His particular and burdensome struggles as a single, unmarried Minister is notable.

www.ingramcontent.com/pod-product-compliance
Lightning Source LLC
Chambersburg PA
CBHW060635290526
45793CB00001B/263